The Australian Aboriginal

The Australian Aboriginal

Text by
ROLAND ROBINSON

Photographs by
DOUGLASS BAGLIN

REED

First published 1968
This edition 1977
A. H. & A. W. REED PTY LTD

53 Myoora Road, Terrey Hills, Sydney
65-67 Taranaki Street, Wellington
11 Southampton Row, London

also at

16 Beresford Street, Auckland
165 Cashel Street, Christchurch

National Library of Australia
Cataloguing in Publication data

Robinson, Roland Edward, 1912-.
  The Australian Aboriginal.

  Bibliography.
  ISBN 0 589 07225 0.

  [1.] Aborigines, Australian. I. Baglin,
  Douglass, photographer. II. Title.

301.451991094

Designed by Publishing Art, Sydney
Set by ASA Typesetters, Sydney
Printed and bound by Everbest Printing Co Ltd, Hong Kong

Contents

Foreword

In writing this story of the Australian Aboriginals one of my aims has been to allow the Aboriginals, as much as possible, to tell the story themselves. Thus much of the text incorporates narratives and accounts, myths and legends, given to me by Aboriginals, as well as personal experiences during many years of field-work, beginning in 1946 with the Djauan tribe on the Roper River, Northern Territory.

Although I have been concerned mainly with collecting the mythology and examples of the art of the Aboriginals, this activity led inevitably into the whole realm of Aboriginal culture, religion, ritual, law and social organisation. Although my instructors and informants have been the Aboriginals themselves, I wish also to acknowledge my indebtedness to the work of Australian anthropologists for considerable help and enlightenment.

The mythology of the Aboriginals is a most illuminating source of knowledge when we attempt to understand their culture, religion, ritual, law and social organisation, and also the origins and the antiquity of the race.

The latter consideration has been one of the reasons why I have been impressed by the theory and relevant facts brought to bear on the coming to Australia by the Aboriginals as expounded by the anthropologist Norman Tindale and the writer H. A. Lindsay. The first chapter of this book, 'The Coming of the Aboriginals', is based on this theory and is supplemented with relevant Aboriginal myths and accounts.

During my field-work throughout Australia I have been impressed by the different physical types of the tribes with whom I have been associated. I found an understanding of these distinct physical types in Mr Tindale's absorbing treatise on the subject.

Some years ago, on Cape York Peninsula, I was puzzled and intrigued by the physical distinction of the Aboriginals I encountered there. Their crinkly hair at first made me suppose that they were descendants of indentured Kanaka labourers. Subsequent inquiries have led me to believe that they are a pocket of surviving Negritoes, the race which Mr Tindale believes inhabited Tasmania. My late friend, the poet and historian Rex Ingamells, a man I greatly respected and admired, also shared this belief regarding the Aboriginal inhabitants of Tasmania.

I am indebted to Mr Douglass Baglin for his interest and collaboration in supplying the photographic plates for this book.

ROLAND ROBINSON

Aboriginals are amongst the world's most ancient peoples. Little is known of them, for they have guarded their past well against their cruel and intolerant invaders of nearly 200 years ago. Today, whilst some investigation is in progress on a scientific level, the average man knows as little of the Aboriginal as did the first settlers.

The race is on now to collect more knowledge—not only by the scientist but by everyone with a sense of observation and respect for the fading remnants of a great people. After a known 31,000 years of occupation in this country, there are few Aboriginals left in the southern states. Most have died of disease. The majority remain in the north, but the drastic impact of extensive mining will soon destroy the last traces of the true full-blood and his wonderful knowledge and understanding of the world and of this continent.

A remarkable people they are, for the average full-blood can speak both his own language and English; he sings, dances, and paints his history and transmits his knowledge through art. He is a remarkable hunter, killing only to eat or for warmth, and he is also a natural conservationist.

A classic example of his understanding of the ecology of his country can be measured by the traces of his long residence of thousands of years on the shores of Sydney Harbour: after that long period the only evidence of his presence was the sight of his fires and canoes. By comparison we, the Europeans, who have been here for less than 200 years have successfully wiped out the last remnants of the local tribes; we have destroyed their environment; and in place of glorious natural forest created a poisonous atmosphere and a polluted harbour around a maze of monstrosities in concrete and steel.

Roland Robinson and I have lived and hunted with the Aboriginals and we hope to pass on the myths and observations of these wonderfully happy times to the average person to help give a renewed interest, pride, and better understanding of a great race of Australian people.

Theirs is a wonderful past, creative and non-destructive; instead of forcing our limited knowledge on to them, let us listen to what they have to say of themselves and of the vast land that they managed so well for an eternity.

My sincere thanks to Peter Baillieu, Geoffrey Goddard, Jeremy Long, Tom Watson, Vic Parkinson, Douglas Belcher and David Goflet who helped in many ways.

DOUGLASS BAGLIN

1 The coming of the Aboriginals

Terra Australis Incognita was the name given by
early cartographers to the imagined and legendary
southern land-mass that we now call Australia. One
of these early maps appears in Cornelius de Jode's
Atlas of 1593, *Speculum Orbis Terrae*, which shows
the northern part of Australia embellished with
ranges of mountains, pictures of a dragon, a lion, and
a serpent, and a hunter armed with bow and arrows.
The sea is decorated with a ship in full sail, sea
monsters, and a merman and a mermaid.

Another map, Cornelius Wytfliet's *Descriptionis Ptolemaicae Augmentum*,
1597, is accompanied by the following passage:

> The terra Australia is therefore the southernmost of all other lands, directly
> beneath the antarctic circle; extending beyond the tropic of Capricorn to the
> West. It ends almost at the equator itself, and separated by a narrow strait,
> lies on the East opposite to New Guinea, only known so far by a few shores
> because after one voyage and another that route has been given up, and
> unless sailors are forced and driven by stress of winds it is seldom visited.
> The terra Australia is said to be of such magnitude that if at any time it is
> fully discovered they think that it will be the fifth part of the world.

Australia, the unknown land, the last of the continents to be discovered by
Europeans, figures in many early records. Marco Polo, visiting the court of
Kublai Khan, obtained information which causes scholars to believe that he had
received knowledge of the Great South Land. The prince of ocean robbers,
Yamada Nagamasa of Japan, with forty pirate vessels, is thought to have landed
on Cape York Peninsula before the days of Tasman. The great maritime
civilisation of the Polynesians must also have known of the continent's shores.

Thousands of years before these early voyages, the ancestors of the Aboriginals
were living in Australia as nomadic Stone Age hunters and food-gatherers. These
early Aboriginals were themselves voyagers and travellers. It is believed that they
had their origins in India, Ceylon and Asia. How then did primitive man
discover and make his home in the Great South Land that was for so long only a
legend to the early European map-makers and navigators?

The answer lies in the emergence of world land-masses during the last Ice Age
when about 75 metres of water was removed from the ocean and piled up as ice
caps on the colder parts of the continents. North-east Asia and America were then
joined where now they are separated by the Bering Strait. This allowed peoples
from north-east Asia to move across to Alaska and spread southwards through the
two American continents.

Australia was then joined to New Guinea and a land bridge connected

Tasmania to the mainland. This permitted the early Aboriginals to follow the archipelago down from Asia, with perhaps some sea crossings by canoes or rafts, to Australia.

It is believed that the Aboriginals were preceded to the continent by the Negritos. Members of this race were seldom more than one and a half metres in height, with hair growing in tight curls. Their original homes were in what are now India, Burma, Thailand, Cambodia and Vietnam. Thousands of years must have passed between the time when the first Negritos were forced to leave their original homes and the arrival of their descendants in Australia.

The Negritos came in two main waves, the first being the early Kartans whose stone tools have been found in many parts of Australia, including Kangaroo Island. The name Kartan has been applied to the early Negritos because 'Karta' was the name given to Kangaroo Island by the later mainland Aboriginals.

Towards the end of the Ice Age another group of Negrito people entered Australia. They used slightly better types of stone implements than the Kartans. They have been named the Tartangans, so called from an island in the lower part of the River Murray where some of their relics and skeletons have been found.

Tartangan type implements have been found in Western Australia and near Lake Menindee, New South Wales. They were mixed with the bones of some of the last giant animals which had lived on in Australia after the close of the Ice Age. The Tartangans made their way into Tasmania, and were living there when the Europeans arrived, but the settlement of Tasmania by the Europeans caused their extinction in this island. A small pocket of Negritos, the Barrineans, still survive on the eastern side of Cape York Peninsula.

Behind the Negritos came the Murrayian Aboriginals. These Aboriginals have been called Murrayian because they were living along the River Murray and its tributaries when Europeans began to settle in Australia. It is believed that the Murrayians' nearest living relations today are the white-skinned Ainu, the Aboriginals of Japan.

A completely different race to the Negritos, the Murrayians are an early form of modern white man. Murrayian men have a heavy growth of hair on their faces, arms, chests, and legs. They are taller and more powerful in build than the little Negritos who preceded them. Their weapons and tools were superior to those of the Negritos. They killed off the little people as they spread southward, and drove them from their country.

Today Murrayians survive mainly along the coast of Western Australia as far north as Broome and Derby, and on the east coast, from Victoria to North Queensland. In their occupation of the continent the Murrayians probably saw the ending of the period of heavy rainfall which followed the last Ice Age.

An invaluable record of the Murrayians was made by the artist George French Angas who visited the colony of South Australia shortly after its founding. As well as painting Aboriginal men, women, and children from life, he provided illustrations of their implements and weapons and baskets, their ceremonial decorations and painting, and provided us with pictures of the country as it was before Europeans had settled there and cleared the forests.

Behind the Murrayians came the Aboriginals known as the Carpentarians. They are a tall race with dark brown skins and with little hair on their faces and bodies. They were the last of the Aboriginals to arrive in Australia. Their surviving relations appear to be the Veddas of Ceylon, and some of the forest tribes of India, Malaya, and Sumatra.

The Carpentarians in their turn had superior weapons and implements to those of the Murrayians. They drove the Murrayians from northern Australia.

A hunter returns to camp with a kangaroo he has speared, carrying it over his shoulders in the traditional manner. In this open plain country near Derby, WA, a hunter can stalk a kangaroo and get to within a few yards of the animal to spear it.

An Aboriginal smearing his hair and body with mud before hunting, done so that the game cannot smell the hunter. From Derby, WA.

This stone in the New England National Park, NSW, is a 'jurraveel' i.e. the site of a totemic ancestor. The stone is of phallic significance and also marks a fertility site.

A study in affection—old man with his dog in a dry river bed near Alice Springs, NT.

The path of a bora ground lined with stones leads to cave paintings near Elsherana, NT.

Preparing for an evening corroboree on Mornington Island, Qld.

An Aboriginal hunting for mudcrabs among the mangroves at Mornington Island.

Aboriginals of Mornington Island enjoy a feed of dugong or sea cow. Traditionally, this food may be hunted only by Aboriginals.

Weapons, implements and a utensil from WA. *Left to right:* A coolamon, a decorated spear-thrower, a boomerang, a spear-thrower, a ritual object, a stone axe, a boomerang. *Bottom:* A hooked boomerang, a stone knife and a scraper.

Still living in tribal states in the large reserves of the Northern Territory, the Carpentarians provide us with the best study of Stone Age Man. Their culture is the richest of all the Aboriginals. For centuries they have been in contact with Malayan, Javanese, and Indonesian visitors and voyagers. The present writer, stepping off the boat at the Port Keats Mission and Reserve, was astounded by the physique of these natives. Many of the men were nearly two metres in height, slender and well proportioned. Many of the women were beautiful creatures, the result of Javanese and Indonesian strains.

Complementary to geological and anthropological knowledge of Australia and its early inhabitants are the myths of the Aboriginals themselves.

One such myth, collected and published by R. H. Mathews in 1899, tells of the voyage to Australia by the ancestors of the Thurrawah tribe. The myth states that in the remote past all the people now in Australia lived in another land beyond the sea. These people decided to leave their own country in canoes and seek fresh hunting grounds which they knew to exist.

The narrative tells how the whale had a large canoe which other members of the tribe stole from him. The whale pursued his tribe across the sea, but the thieves managed to reach Australia ahead of him. They landed at the entrance of Lake Illawarra on the south coast of New South Wales. There the brolga danced in the canoe until a hole was made in it. He then pushed it out a little way from the shore where it was metamorphosed as the island near the entrance. When the whale arrived and saw what had happened he turned back along the coast, where he and his descendants have remained ever since.

Another tradition, this time from the north coast of New South Wales, tells of three brothers and their families who arrived in a sailing ship. They brought with them a steel axe and other possessions from their country in 'the central part of the world'. They anchored at the mouth of the Clarence River and went ashore. During the night a storm drove the ship out to sea and it was never seen again.

The myth tells how the three brothers and their families were forced to remain in Australia. The three brothers, Mamoon, Yar Birrain and Birrung became the founders of three tribes, the Birrein, the Gumbangirr and the Weerluvul. One tribe spread to the north, one to the west, and one to the south. The myth also states that when the three brothers arrived with their families, there were no other humans because the earth had been covered in a great flood.

The coming of the Ice Age affected the climates of the land-masses. Cold winds blowing off the icefields caused shifts of the world's belts of rainfall. A myth of the Dieri tribe of Central Australia tells how these deserts were once lush, fertile areas.

Then, says the myth, instead of the present brazen vault, the sky was covered with clouds so dense that it appeared solid. The air, that is now filled with blinding, salt-laden dust, was washed by soft, cooling rains. At that time the great swamps and lagoons were inhabited by such creatures as the giant lizard Kronosaurus. Huge trees supported a sky of interlacing branches and dense foliage. In this sky-land lived the Kadimakara monsters.

Once, when the Kadimakara had descended from their sky-land to feed on the succulent herbage of the earth, three giant gum-trees, which supported the sky, fell down. The monsters were cut off from their sky-land and forced to roam the earth and wallow in the marshes of Lake Eyre and Lake Callabonna until they died. To this day their bones lie at the place where the monsters died.

After the gum-trees fell down the small holes in the foliage increased in size and number until they touched one another, and the sky became a continuous hole. The sky is called *pura wilpanina*, which means 'great hole'.

The Dieri Aboriginals make journeys to the places where the Kadimakara perished. Rituals are made to appease the spirits of the dead monsters and to persuade them to intercede with those who still dwell in the sky and control the clouds and rain.

This myth is an accurate description of the Permian period when Australia was inhabited by many animals that are now extinct. Among them was the Diprotodon, a wombat-like creature as large as the rhinoceros; the Genyornis, a flightless bird much larger than the emu; and a kangaroo standing over three metres high.

The myth also describes the gradual deterioration of these fertile areas. This happened ten thousand years ago when the climate of the world became warm again, the great icefields melted, and the oceans rose, submerging the land bridges.

It was this account which was the direct cause of the geologist and explorer J. W. Gregory making an expedition to Lake Callabonna in Central Australia. There, as the myth had stated, he found the bones of these prehistoric forms of life. There is at least one complete skeleton of the Diprotodon in the Adelaide Museum, among other exhibits from this area.

When, with the passing of the Ice Age, the oceans slowly rose, submerging the land bridges, Torres Strait reappeared, cutting off New Guinea from the mainland of Australia, Tasmania became an island again, and the flooding of a valley separated Kangaroo Island from the mainland.

In an astonishing manner the myths are again consistent with our scientific knowledge of this past era. All along the coast of New South Wales the various tribes have prevailing myths which speak of geographical changes identical with those brought about by the Ice Age.

An initiated man of the Ngumbarr tribe at Port Macquarie told me that a myth of his people said that at one time all the land in the world was joined up in one big country. Then the big flood came and covered the world. As the water began to go down, the land was divided into continents and islands.

Some people were left on one of these islands. The narrator told me that he thought this 'island' might have been 'that country called Africa'. The people on the island had boomerangs which they threw into the sky and across the water until they disappeared from sight.

One man's boomerang flew on and on until it hit a tree in Australia. Then the people knew that there was land beyond the water that had cut them off. The myth goes on to relate how the people crossed the water and landed on the beach at Middle Head, just down from Macksville.

Yet another initiated man, of the Bunjalung tribe of the Clarence and Richmond Rivers of New South Wales, told me that his myth was a *budgeram*. 'This means,' he said, 'a story of away back in the Beginning'.

'From the Beginning,' the myth commences, this land Australia was one whole land from here to India. The Aboriginals used to go over and fight the Indians, and come back again. The narrator maintained that the old people who handed on this *budgeram* said that the people the Aboriginals fought wore a kind of turban.

On one occasion when the Aboriginals had left their country to fight the Indians, they found, on their way back, that they were cut off by water that spread to the horizon. Their leader caused mountains and islands to rise from the water. With their magico-religious cord, or rope, these Aboriginals crossed the water from island to island until they reached Australia again.

After this the Aboriginals had no further contact with the outside world.

2 The earth-mother

While Europe and Asia experienced successions of earth-exhausting and denuding civilisations, Australia was still a mythical, imagined, unknown land. It had never known the tooth of the plough. It had no blood-written histories of succeeding dynasties, no shattered monuments, tombs, or ruined cities buried beneath exhausted earth and invading sands.

If one looks at Norman Tindale's anthropological map of Australia—Australia as it was before the white man came—it will be seen that the whole continent is portioned out in areas with clearly defined boundaries. These areas are the different countries of the Aboriginal tribes.

It is estimated that when the white man began to settle in Australia there were about 500 different Aboriginal languages in use, and that some 680 tribal groupings existed. It is also estimated that there were about 300,000 Aboriginals living in Australia.

Even the desert regions which appalled and baffled the early explorers, and into which Leichhardt and his expedition vanished without trace, were intimately known to the Aboriginals. Every feature of this vast continent, its rivers, waterholes, ranges, plains covered with grass and abounding with game and bird life, its vast gibber plains and deserts, all were known to the Aboriginals, not only through their nomadic lives of hunting and food-gathering, but through their oral, centuries-old song-cycles and mythological narratives.

The tribal Aboriginal is no scientist. His world is not explained through scientific knowledge. His world is essentially a spiritual one. In these matters he is a poet, an artist, a seer, a sage, a religious patriarch. If he is asked to tell of the nature and significance of his world, it is in these spheres that he will explain it.

And indeed even the scientist becomes something of a poet when he explains 'In the Beginning'. Professor Eddington has written:

> Looking back through the long past we picture the beginning—a primeval chaos which time has fashioned into the universe that we know. Its vastness appals the mind; space boundless though not infinite, according to the strange doctrine of science. The world was almost without form and almost void. But at the earliest state we can contemplate, the void is sparsely broken by tiny electric particles, the germ of the things that are to be, positive and negative they wander aimlessly in solitude, rarely coming near enough to seek or shun one another. They range everywhere so that all space is filled, and yet so empty that in comparison the most highly exhausted vacuum on earth is a jostling throng. In the beginning was vastness, solitude, and the deepest night.

In the Aranda tribe of Central Australia, the term *altjeringa* means 'in the Beginning'. It goes back to a time of chaos and creation from chaos. A myth of the Aranda tribe, transcribed by T. G. H. Strehlow begins:

> In the beginning there was living at Ankota a man who had sprung from the earth without father or mother. He had been lying asleep in the bosom of the earth, and the white ants had eaten his body hollow while the soil rested on him like a coverlet. As he was lying in the ground a thought arose in his mind: 'Perhaps it would be pleasant to arise.' He lay there, deep in thought. Then he arose, out of the soft soil of a little watercourse.

To the Aboriginals, Earth is the great fertility mother. One of the first myths I collected was given to me by the old man Goodoonoo on the Roper River in the Northern Territory. It begins:

> In the Dreamtime the Rainbow Snake came out on to a wide plain ringed by the horizon. There were no trees, no rivers, no grass, anthills, rocks, or anything on this plain, and the Rainbow Snake lay down in the middle of it.
> And the Rainbow Snake had inside herself trees, rocks, animals, birds, and blackfellows. The big snake was rolling about, every way on the ground. She was groaning and calling out. She was making a big noise with all the blackfellows, everything, inside her belly.

But the Rainbow Snake could not give birth until a man came and speared her. Then out of the spear wound fluid poured. From this fluid the billabongs and rivers, the trees, grass and rocks, the animals, reptiles and birds, and the blackfellows were formed.

In another myth from the Roper River the Rainbow Snake is travelling.

> As the Rainbow Snake travelled along she looked back and saw that the winding track she was making was turning into a deep river with trees and reeds and lilies, and, far behind her, she saw billabongs gleaming in the sun. And again she looked back and saw all the bush and the mountains rising behind her. 'What is happening?' said the Rainbow Snake. 'How am I doing this?'

Creative journeys abound in Aboriginal mythology. At least two that are known to the writer have crossed the continent, one from the south (Port Augusta) to the north (Darwin), the other from Byron Bay, New South Wales, to the *borrgorr*, the sea where the sun sets. These creative journeys were made by ancestral beings, both men and women. Ancestral beings not only created the features of the continent as they travelled, but also carried and distributed objects which were the sources of ritual and tribal law as well as the sources of all forms of life, including the Aboriginals themselves.

In the north a most important ancestral being is Kunapipi. She is a fertility goddess. The name means 'old woman'. She is the earth mother. She rose out of the sea like the Greek goddess Aphrodite, at the mouth of the Roper River. The Kunapipi myth and ritual are widely distributed in the northern part of the continent.

Associated with Kunapipi in the north is the Rainbow Serpent. This ancestral being, one would say, was continent-wide in ritual and mythology. In recent years I have learned of its existence in New South Wales as well as in the central and northern areas. The Bunyip, always believed to be associated with the Rainbow Serpent, is called Warwai in New South Wales—a name in that area for the Rainbow Serpent.

In this group of ancestral beings the Djanggawul, two men and two women, and the Djankawau, should be mentioned. The Djankawau, who were two sisters, came, according to the myth, from Buralku, the Island of the Spirits of the Dead, which lies somewhere in the northern-eastern sea.

The two sisters did not originate there, but it is there that the myth begins with the two sisters making a canoe and filling it with *rangga*, or ritual objects. The two sisters set out from the island, and the morning star threw its ray of light across the water, showing them the way. They followed the direction the sun 'walked' over the sky. A fish swam before the canoe, continually leaping out of the water as it led them on. Day and night the sisters paddled the canoe until they reached the mainland. They were covered with dried salt spray, the impregnating life of the sea.

The two sisters took all their *rangga* out of the canoe and left it on the beach. The canoe itself is a mother symbol. The sisters travelled inland, leaving behind them at various places their *rangga*, which became the sources of various forms of life, including human beings. As they travelled the sisters made ritual totemic wells or centres with their yam-sticks.

Eventually, while the sisters were away gathering food, men came and stole their dillybags, which they had left hanging in a tree. The bags contained their *rangga* of ritual. The sisters returned and found the *rangga* gone. Then they heard the sound of the ritual that the men were making. The sisters covered their ears and said, 'We cannot hear this ritual. It belongs to the men. Now we must bear children and look after them, and gather food.'

Another myth that illustrates the nature and significance of ancestral beings, together with their sacred ritual objects, is one which Albert Namatjira, the painter of the Aranda tribe in Central Australia, gave me. Its outline is as follows:

An old man started out from a cave in Haast's Bluff (another mother symbol). He carried with him a *tjurunga*, a flat, oval inscribed stone, which contained the old man's indestructible spirit, and six *namatoona*, smaller copies of his *tjurunga*, in a dillybag hanging from his neck.

The six *namatoona* were his sons. If he wanted game, he would take out the six *namatoona*, rub some goanna fat on them, and the *namatoona* would stand up as his six sons. The old man would give each son a spear and a womerah, and his sons would go out hunting.

The six sons fed only from the old man's blood. (Here again is the mother significance.) The old man would open a vein in his arm, fill a hollow womerah with his blood, and give it to his sons.

When the old man came to a camp where there were women, he told them that he had six sons to give them in marriage. In the night the old man got up and took the *namatoona* out of the hair of each of his sons and put them back in his dillybag.

Early in the morning the old man travelled away from the camp, and when the women woke, the six sons were gone. They could find only the tracks of the old man. The women went after him and questioned him about his sons. The old man eluded their questions by saying, 'They might have gone out hunting', or 'They might be back at the camp.' Those women never found the six sons.

The old man travelled on, repeating this performance. Then when the old man got tired and old, he died. He made his camp and lay down and put his dillybag alongside him. When the old man was dead, the six *namatoona* in the dillybag wanted to get out. They started to roll about in the dillybag, and the dillybag rolled round and round in a circle.

The old man turned into stone. Underneath that stone is a big *tjurunga* belonging to the old man. And near him is a black stone which is the dillybag with the six *namatoona* inside.

Creative journeys of ancestral beings are not to be considered merely in the physical sense. To the Aboriginals the features of their landscapes are of a spiritual nature. Thus, in the outline of the last myth, the metamorphoses of the old man and his six sons as certain stones in the landscape establish a feature which would be impregnated and potent with the ancestral being's spirit.

A woman conceiving a child in any part of the country nearest to this totemic centre would be considered to have received the spirit of her child from this site. Thus the child's totem would be decided. The site would be the spiritual home of the child to which it would return after death.

Any country of an Aboriginal tribe abounds in such sites. Apart from hunting and food-gathering rights, it is essentially such features of the landscape which determine the country of individuals and the tribe.

An excellent example of an ancestral being creating such sites, and a clear illustration of their sacred nature and the operation of their potency was given to me by the old Mardinga of the Murinbata tribe at Port Keats in the Northern Territory:

> In the place called Nimaluk where spring-water is bubbling up, the Rainbow Snake made a wide, clear space. In this place he set out lines of stones. He said, 'These stones I put out in a dry place. These stones contain the spirits of my men-children. They are *ngarit-ngarit*, the spirit-children. All my girl-children, the *murinbungo* I will keep with me in the water. I put the name Kooranimaluk to this spring-water. We cannot lose this country. We stop here. We watch this place called Nimaluk.'
>
> In another place the Rainbow Snake made a big, clear space again. He set stones all round this place. He said, 'In these stones are the spirits of my fish-children, *wallamun*, the mullet.' And in other places he set stones for his spirit-children, *pulangar*, the dingo; *ninno*, the tortoise; and *kirick*, the goose.
>
> An old man camped near the place Nimaluk. He found plenty of food there, fish, goanna, tortoise and yam. The Rainbow Snake sent out a big light from the bubbling water. In the light from the water he sent a spirit-child to that old man's wife. When the child was born, it was a girl. Everyone said, 'oh, what a pretty girl,' 'oh, what good hair this girl has'. The old man said, 'The Rainbow Snake has sent his child from the water.'
>
> The spirit-child may be in a fish, goanna, tortoise, or a goose, or anything that is speared for food. When this food is taken back to the camp, the spirit-child goes into a woman there. It goes in under her toenail, and goes up inside that woman.
>
> Moitta was born with a crooked arm because his brother had been out hunting and had speared a goose with a *ngarit-ngarit* inside it. He broke the goose's wing and took it back to the camp. The spirit-child inside the goose went into his mother and was born as Moitta with the crooked arm.

This account also explains the tie, indeed one might say the umbilical cord, by which an Aboriginal is attached to his or her country.

The continent was known to the Aboriginals not only through the oral traditions of the creative journeys of ancestral beings, but also by their traditional trade routes. Trade, to the Aboriginal, has a different motivation and value than it has to the white man. To the Aboriginal it is an activity through which he fulfils his tribal obligations and maintains his status in the tribe.

North-eastern Arnhem Land is still a centre of ceremonial trade or exchange. The late Dr Donald Thomson, in his investigation of the activity in this area, showed that such articles as axes, iron, wire, calico and tobacco, brought by early Macassan voyagers, passed south and west from Arnhem Land into the continent on traditional trade routes.

Articles such as boomerangs, not made and used in Arnhem Land, ironwood hook spears, and bamboo spearshafts, passed northwards from the Katherine and Daly Rivers into Arnhem Land. From the Walker River of Blue Mud Bay in the Gulf of Carpentaria, highly valued flint spearheads spread throughout eastern Arnhem land to the south beyond the Roper River, and to the west across the Liverpool River.

From the Kimberley district in the north of Western Australia the beautifully made, pressure-flaked, and serrated-edged stone spearheads passed down into the centre of Australia in return for red ochre. *Pituri*, a tobacco-like plant, red ochre, stone axeheads knives and spearheads, passed up and down a traditional trading route from the coastal Aboriginals in South Australia along the Cooper River and the Strzelecki Track into western Queensland.

The site of the Lutheran Mission of Kopperamanna, between Maree and Birdsville, was known to be a traditional meeting ground for trade.

To the early European explorers and settlers, Australia was often a country of deception, mirage and illusion. Engulfing silences reached out beyond the normal range of sound, clarifying it, dampening the echo, so that a man shouting, the howl of a dingo, or the most profound uttered wisdom appeared of no account. This was the country recorded in the explorer Edward John Eyre's diary, an account which, when his wife read it, caused her hair to turn white in a single night.

This is the country whose every feature was intimately known to the Aboriginals. It was known to them through their nomadic lives of hunting and food-gathering, their traditional trading routes, the diffusion of their religious cults, and the oral traditions of their ancestral beings' creative journeys.

This 'barren accurst land' was, to the Aboriginals, their fertility mother, their home from the creation time. An Aboriginal's reverence for, and fierce pride in, his 'country' was expressed to me by a man of the Djauan tribe on the Roper River. He was a stockman on a cattle station which occupied his 'country'. He said, 'Because you come here, build stockyard, bring cattle, make homestead, this is not your country. Every plain, rock, water-hole, belong to my people right back to Dreamtime.'

3 Hunting and food-gathering

The Aboriginal is finely attuned to Nature. He is part of the balance of Nature. Civilisation is only a veneer, a facade. Modern man has been called the new barbarian. Judged by his behaviour in the world today and in the past, and compared with the Aboriginal, he is an anarchic barbarian. He has caused the great rupture with Nature. He violates and destroys the mother earth. He eliminates all living creatures other than those which he can domesticate, or which serve him. Space-age man already thinks in terms of occupying some other planet, and, presumably, starting the whole process again.

Such thinking, behaviour and values are alien to the nature of the tribal Aboriginals. As hunters and gatherers of food they have a reverence for the earth mother who provides them with sustenance. Their laws forbid any violation or unrestrained greed. In contrast, modern man has conquered Nature and regards the fertility of the earth and its resources as wealth which he can possess, sell and exhaust, and which he can have represented as figures in his bank balance. As D. H. Lawrence remarked, 'The mosquito may drink your blood, but he does not put it in the bank.'

An illustration of the awe in which Aboriginals regard the sources of food is provided by the myth of Garun the Turtle. This myth was related to me by a tribesman called Mungi in north-eastern Arnhem Land.

Two men set out in their canoe from Elcho Island to hunt turtle. They speared a turtle, put in at a beach and cut up the turtle on the sand. The shell, bones and skin they left on the shore. The spirit of the turtle spoke, 'All right, I leave my bones and shell here. My spirit goes back to live in the Saltwater.'

The two men took the turtle-meat and paddled away along the shore. Two turtles came out of the jungle and began to lay their eggs in the sand on a beach. One of the turtles was Garun the turtle ancestress. The two men beached their canoe, and one of them killed Garun as she was laying her eggs. They made a fire and cooked and ate the turtle.

Then the spirit of Garun the turtle spoke, 'You two men have killed my body. But you cannot kill my spirit. I will go now to stay in the Saltwater at my country Gooraya.'

Then the two men got in their canoe again and paddled away. They came to the country of Garun. The spirit of Garun saw the two men coming. As they paddled up to the beach, the spirit of Garun made a big fire. Then the men in the canoe saw a huge sea coming up behind them. They ran their canoe up on to the sand. As they did so the spirit of Garun took a firestick and

Aboriginal climbing coconut palm to collect coconuts on Groote Eylandt, Gulf of Carpentaria.

Aboriginal girls collecting yams while the men are hunting. Groote Eylandt, NT.

Aboriginal of Derby, WA, eating the delicacy of
roast kangaroo tail.

An Aboriginal hunter on the Mitchell River,
Qld, with two wallabies and a brolga, the large
Australian crane.

Turtle is a great delicacy for
the Aboriginals on
Mornington Island, Qld.

Fruit segments of the pandanus palm are much favoured by the Aboriginals. The red segments contain small nuts; note paperbark dish. Arnhem Bay, NT.

The first phase of cooking a kangaroo. The hair is burned off and the animal then cooked in a ground oven lined with stones, in which a small fire has burned down to the embers. The oven containing the kangaroo is covered with a sheet of bark and heaped over with earth.

Cycad palm with nuts. These nuts are gathered by women for food at Arnhem Bay, NT. After leaching in water the nuts are ground between stones, mixed with water and made into cakes or a kind of damper baked in the fire.

Aboriginal hunting with a gun in the open country near Derby, WA. Europeans are teaching them their skills.

Fishing in mud holes with a net in mangrove swamps on Mornington Island, Gulf of Carpentaria. These nets are made from fig-tree bark fibre.

came down on the canoe. The canoe went up in one huge blaze and roar. The sea reared up and crashed over the two men. It swallowed them, drowned them.

On the beach the spirit of Garun spoke: 'Look, you two men, you killed my body in another country. My bones and shell stayed on that shore. You came here to kill my spirit. Now my spirit has killed you.'

This myth is an example of the Aboriginal attitude towards hunting and obtaining food. Enough should be taken to satisfy immediate needs. The two hunters whose selfishness drove them to attempt to destroy a source of life and fertility suffered the fate they deserved.

There are many such myths of this nature. They show the reverence and regard the Aboriginals have for the earth mother in all phases of her fertility, and the contempt they have for those possessed by unnatural greed.

With regard to hunting and food-gathering, an Aboriginal tribe is divided by the sexes. The man is the hunter, the woman the gatherer of food. If a tribal group is camped for a length of time, the men set out early in the morning with their spears and womerahs. The women and children set out in a different direction with their coolamons, dillybags and digging-sticks. If a family or tribal group is on the move the men will walk ahead carrying their spears and womerahs, constantly on the alert for game to be speared or stalked. The women and children follow with their possessions, often carrying the very small children.

On several occasions on the Roper River I accompanied an Aboriginal named Nalul when he went out hunting for wallabies, to see for myself how they were stalked and speared. Like Nalul, I was barefooted, the soles of my feet hardened through months of going about without shoes. Like this, I was nearer to Nalul's quiet tread moving over dry leaves and grass and, like him, made no crunching and clatter moving over stony stretches.

We came to lightly timbered plain country of tall dry grass and red-and-black termite formations. The Aboriginals do not like hunting wallabies on windless days. For reasons of scent and sound, it is then difficult to get within spearing distance.

We began to face into a light wind. I was a little behind Nalul, who held one spear in his womerah in readiness, and in his left hand carried his second spear.

The grass through which we were moving was more than waist high and sometimes, ahead and to the side of us, a wallaby would bound up, making his first two or three loud thumps as he went off.

Suddenly, I was startled by a wallaby that bounded up about fifteen yards ahead of us. I saw Nalul's spear arm go over. The spear hurtled and writhed through the air impelled by the force with which the womerah had driven it. The spear took the wallaby just beside and in the middle of his backbone. The wallaby was still bounding through the grass with the spear apparently still in him. Soon we could not see the animal over the tall grass.

'We track him,' said Nalul, pointing to the sharp claw marks and spurts of earth where the wallaby had bounded away. 'He lay down that way,' and Nalul pointed with his lips to a nest-like place in the grass.

We followed the wallaby through grass and over open spaces where I could see no track but where Nalul could show me a displaced stick or broken grass stem, or even a bent grass stem that was slowly righting itself. Before long we came on the exhausted wallaby. Nalul carried it back to camp by throwing it over his shoulder and holding it by the hind legs.

On another day I saw Nalul approach to within eight metres of a wallaby to spear it. We were in lightly grassed country abounding with red termite formations. On sighting the wallaby, Nalul arrested his walk and signed with his left hand for me to continue in the direction I was going. The attention of the wallaby, which was some distance off, was attracted by me as I walked on.

Glancing sideways, I watched Nalul taking every advantage of termite formations, every sparse tree. At the slightest sign of apprehension on the wallaby's part, he arrested whatever action he was taking and became one with his surroundings.

At last I saw the brown, tense figure take his stand. With legs apart, arm and womerah drawn back full length, and the three-metre spear at about the level of his eyes, Nalul hurled the weapon with savage force and aim. The spear took the wallaby in the ribs.

Back at the camp the wallaby was thrown down and cooked in the following manner. A hollow deep enough to accommodate the animal was scooped in the sandy earth. This hollow was lined with river stones. A reasonably small fire was made in the hollow and allowed to burn down to coals and ash.

By this time the internal organs of the wallaby had been removed, its hind and forelegs bent and bound to its body and, unskinned, the wallaby was ready for cooking. Some of the hot stones from the fire were put inside the carcase, together with some eucalyptus leaves for flavouring. The wallaby was placed in the ground oven and sprinkled with water. More hot stones were placed over the wallaby, and then the oven was covered with a sheet of paperbark and mounded over with earth.

This kind of ground oven produces a great heat, as can be found by placing one's hand on the mound or being present at the conclusion of the cooking when the covering of earth and paperbark is removed, and the steaming, well-cooked and flavoured wallaby is revealed.

The wallaby is shared by the tribal group, but it is the right of the old men to name and receive any part of the wallaby they feel like eating.

On another occasion, I was talking to the tribesman Ongi as he sat under a figtree painting his spearblade in a cross-hatched design with red ochre and white pipeclay. He asked me if I had noticed that the native plum-tree, called *woial*, was beginning to flower.

'When the plum-tree comes into flower,' said Ongi, 'we know that the rain-time is close up. And then Dooruk, the emu, will come looking for plums. He comes to the plum-tree and kicks the trunk with his foot. The plums fall down and Dooruk runs about under the tree pecking them up. He makes this drumming sound in his chest—*duk-duk-duk*.

'A man finds a tree that Dooruk always comes to when he is looking for plums. He sees the emu's tracks all round the tree. During the night he climbs into the tree with his spear, womerah and club. He sits up in the boughs and leaves waiting for Dooruk.

'The tribesmen have been hunting Dooruk in the rain-time and this has made Dooruk frightened. When it is little-bit daylight Dooruk comes after the plums. The man in the tree keep still. He hears the emu as he walks in circles round the tree. *Duk-duk*, he says now and again. Dooruk is hungry for the plums, but he thinks that someone may be hiding in the tree, waiting to spear him.

'The tree is quiet. Dooruk can see the plums lying on the ground underneath the tree. He circles in closer and closer, craning his neck, and peering into and under the tree with his red eyes.

'At last Dooruk can wait no longer. The tree is dark and quiet. Suddenly, he runs right in underneath the boughs. *Duk-duk-duk*, he talks as he walks about pecking up the plums.

'The man in the tree has his spear hooked up in his womerah. Without touching a leaf he draws back his arm with the spear and spear-thrower. He knows where he must spear Dooruk, in the thigh joint, cutting the big sinew.

'He waits and watches Dooruk. Suddenly the spear comes down like lightning out of the boughs. It finds Dooruk's thigh joint and cuts through the sinew.

'Dooruk falls to the ground. He flounders about, crying out with guttural cries. He is beating his wings, trying to get up. The man drops out of the tree with his club. Dooruk strikes at him with his long neck and strong beak. The man dodges the striking head. He runs in and clubs Dooruk behind his angry red eyes. Dooruk tries to rear up. His wings beat the air. He falls down, and his body shudders. He stiffens out his legs and shakes his feet.

'That's how we must hunt the emu in the rain-time,' said Ongi as he made with his sliver of bark the last, delicate line of white clay down his sharp iron spearblade.

About this time the paperbark trees were in flower alongside the river and the flying foxes had arrived. During the day they hung upside down in bunches and lines from the high branches of the trees. They came to the trees about daylight, filling the morning with their myriad, shrill screams, after having been out all night feeding on the nectar of distant flowering trees.

About sunset they would leave the trees overhanging the river and stream down, dipping themselves in the water, and then hang upside down in the trees again, licking the water off their bodies before setting out for their night's feeding.

The time of the flying foxes' flights down the river was the time for the Aboriginals to procure them for food. The men would plaster themselves over with mud, so that flying foxes could not smell them, they told me. Then with long, pliant sticks they climbed into the smaller trees crowding and overhanging the river.

The Aboriginals were hidden by the thick foliage with only their long sticks held upright showing. As the flying foxes streamed down from the trees, and over the surface of the water, the pliant sticks got to work. Swish, swish, thump, thump, the sticks came down, knocking the flying foxes into the water. There they were seized and retrieved by the Aboriginals' dogs.

The two species of flying foxes, the red and the black, were fat and succulent from feeding on the flowering trees. Lightly roasted on the fire, they provided an almost uninterrupted fare for the Aboriginals during the season of the flying foxes.

These Aboriginals had dogs of mystifying breeds, cross-bred from our introduced dogs. The dingo, Australia's only non-marsupial animal, was a hunting dog. We believe that it was brought to the continent by the Aboriginals and then went wild. An old Aboriginal woman on the Roper River told me that they used to have tame native cats. She told me that the Aboriginals sent their native cats up into the trees to hunt possums for them.

On the Roper River and throughout the Northern Territory the water-lily, both the purple and the red 'lotus lily', are sources of food. When the flower dies it forms a dense knob of seeds. The women grind them between grinding stones. The ground meal is made into a dough, formed into small cakes, and baked in the ashes of the fire. These cakes have the dense consistency of rye bread, and I found them tasty and sustaining.

The long, pale-green stems of the water-lily, which reach up from the mud to the surface of the water, are eaten. They are stripped as one would strip celery, eaten raw, and are not unlike celery in taste.

When the water-lilies die off their bulbs remain in the deep mud of the billabongs and rivers. I have gathered these bulbs with children and women. It is a pleasant occupation. You wade into the billabong, sometimes up to your thighs or waist, and feel about in the deep mud with your hands and feet. When you have a couple of handfuls of bulbs you call to your nearest companion who pushes the boat-like coolamon over the water to you. You put your bulbs in the little vessel and give it a push to send it across to someone else.

Within an hour, the coolamon has been emptied on to the bank several times and you have also found quite a number of mussels. When you and your Aboriginal companions wade out of the billabong and wash the blue mud off your legs there is quite a pile of lily bulbs and mussels on the bank to be shared and carried back to the camp.

Back at the camp the bulbs are roasted in the fire like chestnuts, and are not unlike them in taste. These, together with yams, a tuber dug out of the ground, or a wallaby, or a goanna or two, or perhaps fish, provide a satisfying meal for Aboriginals on the Roper River.

Fish are speared in this river and in the nearby billabongs. I once saw Ongi come into camp with a huge barramundi. He held it over his shoulder by the gills, and its tail brushed the ground.

This was in the dry time of the year, when the water level falls in the billabongs and the barramundi are trapped. The Aboriginals know where they are and take them when they are ready for them. The barramundi is a handsome, voracious fish which has been known to reach a weight of over 40 kilograms in Northern Territory rivers. He travels right up these rivers to their sources. White men and Aboriginals alike say that the barramundi is 'number one tucker'.

The rivers and billabongs abound in other fish: a kind of black bream, the rifle fish (which often obtains its food by coming to the surface and spurting a series of water pellets at insects clinging to reeds and leaves), catfish and rainbow fish.

I have gone out with the Aboriginals to hunt for tortoises. A line of men wades into a billabong. They dive and swim under water in line, surface, and dive again, moving up the billabong and catching the tortoises as they go.

At the time of the year when the fallen pollen of the acacias covers many of the river reaches and billabongs with a golden skin, the crocodiles come out and lay their eggs in sandy places on the banks. The Aboriginals find the places that are marked by the feet of the crocodile and the circular movements of their tails. The large imprint of the belly plates can be seen where they lay their eggs. The crocodile, like the turtle and the tortoise, digs down into the sand, lays her eggs, fifteen or so in number, covers the place, and leaves the eggs for the sun to incubate.

We found the eggs exceptionally good to eat, especially when garnished with slices of onion and made into a large omelette. These eggs, like those of the turtle and tortoise, are part of the Aboriginals' fare.

On one occasion when on the Daly River, I set out in the evening with a party of Aboriginals to obtain pied and pygmy geese. The men had provided themselves with bundles of green sticks for throwing. We waded the river crossing and went a short distance to a swamp. In the half darkness the geese were flying down to the swamp. They could be seen against the light in the sky as they came into the swamp.

At throwing height the geese were brought down by the sticks hurled by the hunters, who were hidden in the reeds and scrub. Sometimes the hunters would imitate the cries of the birds, calling them to where they waited with their throwing-sticks.

As well as spearing fish, the Aboriginals constructed weirs of bushes, or traps of stones across river-beds. A myth related to me by Tjonba of the Aranda tribe in Central Australia tells of this method when the dry watercourses were suddenly flooded from distant rains in the Gulf country and in the north.

The fish-woman Intabidna travelled from Loowarra, the big waterhole. She went past the running water Etmungarra. She went across the big plain Ilduraba, which is dotted with little round stones. These stones are *quadda*, the eggs that the fish-woman left. She came from the south and she was travelling towards Indareya, which is Hermansburg Mission.

As she travelled she sang, 'I see that claypan far ahead of me. I think there is water there. No more. That water has gone away.' That water was vanishing water, mirage.

She travelled on and came to Uratanga, a big water. It can't dry. It can never finish. It is quicksand. A big sandhill is there. The white man calls it salt-hole.

At Uratanga a mob of blacks made a big V-shaped weir out of bushes. They made this fish-trap called *unjea*. They caught a big mob of fish. One big fish they could not catch; it was too cunning. That fish was the woman-fish. She was woman, *kunga*. She had a woman's head, breasts, arms and body. Her body ended in a fish's tail.

The old man called out, 'Hey, that one is Intabidna the woman-fish! She runs away!'

The woman-fish went back to her country. That woman-fish was my grandmother. Her name was Palabultjura.

The sandhill in this myth is, of course, the metamorphosis of the fish-trap.

Fish nets over three metres long are woven by the Aboriginals from fig-tree bark-cord and other bark fibres. These are used as seines in the waterholes and rivers.

A famous stone fish-trap, or at least its remains, is in the Barwon River at Brewarrina, New South Wales. It was a maze of low stone walls in the river bed. Mrs Doreen Wright, an Aboriginal woman of Brewarrina, has this to say of the fish-trap:

Old King Clyde (a tribal elder), he was the boss of the stone fish-traps here in the river at Brewarrina. When the old people wanted to get fish down at the traps, the old King would tell them all to stand out on the banks.

The old King would dive into the water. He would talk to the fish, telling them to go into the stone fish-trap. The old people wouldn't have to spear the fish, they could just walk into the water and catch them under the gills, and fill their *bugguda*, their dillybags up with them.

'*Ngimbi durriai*', that old King would talk. That means, 'Wait here now. I go in to get the fish.'

A caste-Aboriginal of the Bunjalung tribe told me the porpoises used to help the Aboriginals in their fishing. 'When the season of the sea-mullet was in,' he said, 'the old people would go down to the river and beat their spears on the water. The school of porpoises would come and chase the schools of sea-mullet right into the shallow water, ankle-deep, where the old people used to get just enough for two or three meals without wasting any. The old people used to tell us that when we went fishing, we should spear just enough for our needs, without wasting any.'

Malcolm River, an Aboriginal from the south coast of New South Wales, told me how he had seen duck caught.

> The tribe used to make nets out of rushes. They would stretch the nets across a big creek to stop the ducks coming down. Then they would go up to the top of the creek and hunt the ducks down. They'd throw their boomerangs whistling in the air over the ducks to drive them down into the nets stretched across the creek. Those ducks, flying low over the water, would hit the net and break their necks.
>
> That's the truth. That's the finish. That's the way they did it in the old times. I've seen it done myself.

And finally, here is an old friend of mine, Percy Mumbulla, telling me about a great fisherman in his tribe.

> Old Billy Bulloo was a clever old man. He would never go out fishing on a calm day. But if the sea was rough, mountains high, he would jump in his canoe and get his fish by spearing them. He could see the fish in the waves.
>
> A mullet, he never travels in the calm. He waits for the wind to blow a gale. Soon as ever he feels that wind on him—cold—he jumps out of the water. He's feeling for that westerly wind. When that wind blows, you see the water black with leaping mullet, thousands and thousands of leaping mullet.
>
> That's when old Billy Bulloo used to get his fish.

4 Weapons and implements

'The red flying foxes and black flying foxes were once
men. They cut and shaved down acacia wood for
their spears. They cut a bone-barb. They planed a flat
place on the spear-blade, on which to lay the barb.
With fig-tree string they bound on the barb. They
painted their spears with red clay and white clay.
They carried their spears on their shoulders.'

This opening of a myth from the Munkun tribe on Cape York Peninsula
describes how, in the Dreamtime, the flying-fox men made their spears. Another
narrative from the Roper River speaks of the introduction of the spear-thrower to
the Aboriginals in the Dreamtime.

When Koopoo, the red plain kangaroo, made his creative journey across
Arnhem Land from the Timor Sea to the Gulf of Carpentaria in the Dreamtime,
one of his companions was Waarlark, the flying fox.

'Waarlark wanted to show the tribesmen how to make and use the spear-
thrower, but the tribesmen said they like to throw the spear without the
womerah. And Koopoo did not want the tribesmen to learn how to make and use
the spear-thrower. But still, Waarlark showed the tribesmen how to make and use
it. This is why Waarlark has the spur, or the hook of the spear-thrower, on the end
of his arm.'

A tradition from the New England district of New South Wales also speaks of
tribes which did not use the spear-thrower. 'Their shields, *buggarr*, came from
the central part of the world. Also their spears. They never used the woomera, the
spear-thrower. They threw the spear with only their hand, holding the spear in
the middle.'

The spear-thrower and the spear may be likened to the bow and its arrow, or the
rifle and its ammunition. The spear-thrower is usually about a metre long. The
Roper River one is made of ironwood, flat, smooth, about five centimetres wide,
and tapering at its hooked end. The other end is shaped for the handgrip. The
hook, or spur, against which the hollow end of the spear-shaft fits, is fastened on
with hardened gum or resin.

To throw the spear, the spear-thrower and spear-shaft are gripped with one
hand. The three-metre spear is sometimes held up with the extended left forearm
or wrist. When the spear is hurled, the spear-thrower is retained in the hand. The
spear-thrower's metre-long extension to the throwing arm, and the fact that the
spear is propelled from the end of its shaft, gives the weapon considerable
impetus and range.

The spear-thrower is also used as a weapon to ward off or deflect spears in
fighting when a man's spears are expended. In such cases the tribesman may
recover spears hurled against him and, with his spear-thrower, hurl them back at

his opponents. The sharpened end of the spear-thrower can also be used as a stabbing weapon or a digging-stick.

At Port Keats in the Northern Territory most of the tribe took part in a contest to demonstrate how far a spear could be hurled. They used light mangrove spears. I did not step out the distance, which ended in mangroves, but it seemed something like 275 metres. The heavier and longer spear would not be thrown this distance. I once asked a Roper River tribesman to demonstrate his accuracy with the spear. Without seeming to take aim, and without undue force, he embedded his iron-blade spear in the thick bark of a gum-tree some forty-five metres off.

The spear-thrower of Central Australian tribes is wide, almost an oval, and concave. It can be used for carrying food, or fire coals. It will be recalled that, in the myth of the wandering ancestor of the Aranda tribe, the old man fed his sons by filling his womerah with his blood and letting his sons eat from it.

Spears used in north-eastern Arnhem Land may be divided into four main types, according to each type of spearhead. They are the stone, the wooden, the sting-ray prong and the iron.

The stone-flaked spearhead is normally fifteen centimetres long, but varies from seven to seventeen centimetres. Flaked stone spearheads are made in this area, but the beautiful, pressure-flaked spearheads with serrated edges come into this area along trade routes from the Kimberley region in Western Australia. The spear-shafts are usually of eucalypt, but bamboo shafts are used, these shafts coming along trade routes from the south.

The art of the stone spearhead maker was once explained to me by an old man of the Djauan tribe.

> The spearhead maker has an assistant who is allowed to do all the preliminary labouring work. This consists in going with the 'master' to the quarry, splitting the boulder with fire, or splitting off the portion of stone selected by the craftsman, from the mass, with fire.
>
> When the stone is ready for the spearhead maker, the assistant may participate no further. Squatting down, the craftsman splits the fragment to its required shape with wooden wedges and stone hammer. With a stone hammer he strikes out the long spearhead flakes complete from the stone. As he strikes them off he stands them in a long line in the sand beside him. On one side of him is a line of smooth spearheads. On the other side are the irregular ones. The smooth ones are for fighting, the irregular ones are for hunting.
>
> These spearheads are carefully bound in paperbark and traded by the spearhead maker to natives who come from distant countries for either fighting or hunting spearheads.

Pressure-flaked spearheads are a consummate Stone Age art. Those I have seen and handled were made from a milky, semi-transparent quartz, and some from clear window-glass; one small one was made from brown bottle-glass. I was also told that the Aboriginals would break the porcelain insulators on telegraph lines for spearhead material.

These particular spearheads are the shape of a symmetrical eucalyptus leaf. They are flaked to serrated edges from a fine spine running down the centre of each side of the spearhead to a skin-pricking sharp point. The symmetry of these spearheads represents the art of a master craftsman in any age.

A stone spearhead is fitted to the shaft of the spear by splitting the distal end to allow the spearhead to be inserted. The shaft and base of the spearhead are then

Opposite
The traditional method of making a fire. Groote Eylandt, Gulf of Carpentaria.

A temporarily abandoned paperbark-covered dwelling near the beach at Smith Point, Port Essington, NT.

An Aboriginal man from Groote Eylandt making rope used in dugong and turtle hunting.

An Aboriginal spearing fish off shore at Yirrkala, NT. The fish spear, with three iron or wire tines, is hooked up in the throwing-stick in readiness.

Bathurst Island, NT. Aboriginals finishing off a Macassar-type canoe carved from a single tree-trunk. Note blocks left inside for stepping the mast.

Framework of an old Aboriginal dwelling on Yandama Station, near Milparinka, NSW. These dwellings were originally covered with bark, branches, or grass. The axemarks on the timber could be made by a stone axe.

A Bathurst Islander carves a canoe out of a solid log—with an axe.

bound with fibre string and coated with beeswax. The wooden-headed spear has several types:

1 The mangrove spear is an unbarbed sharpened stick about two and a half metres long. It is used both for fighting and hunting in mangrove jungles.
2 The unbarbed spear with wooden head is of hardwood and is also used for hunting and fighting. It is about thirty-three centimetres in length.
3 A one-pronged wooden spear with barbs on one side. A sub-type of this spear has its barbs only partly carved through its head, a series of parallel perforations continuing the demarcation of the barb, and creating a lace-like appearance. These spears are usually made of ironwood. They are bound to the shaft with fibre cord and cemented with resin, and the propelling ends of the spears are also bound with string and coated with beeswax or resin.
4 A spear with a much larger head, about seventy-five to eighty centimetres long. It may be barbed on one or both sides, its barbs opposed. When this spear is used it is most difficult to withdraw.
5 A bilaterally barbed spear with two prongs, each with small barbs on only one side of each prong, used for fighting and duelling.
6 A two- to four-pronged spear with barbs cut on both sides of the prongs. This spear is used for fishing.
7 The stingray spear made by coastal natives. Barbed prongs found on the tail of a stingray are kept by the hunter. He attaches twelve to thirty, arranged in a semicircular set of points, to a two-metre shaft.

The iron spearhead, the 'shovel nose', may be thirty centimetres long. Those I have seen in use appeared to have been made from various pieces of iron, perhaps from ships or old machinery. Sometimes they had rivet-holes in them and had obviously been beaten out and ground down to the shape required. They are not unlike a heavy knifeblade, sharpened on both edges. They can be detached from the spear-shaft and used as a knife.

Thick wire or iron rods, are used by the Aboriginals, when they can be obtained, to make their four-pronged fishing spears.

The spear has its ritual and mythical associations. In the Aranda myth of the Seven Sisters (the Pleiades), their amorous and creative pursuer, the old man Yoola (Orion), carries a spear which is undoubtedly of phallic significance. When Yoola camped, he stood his spear upright in the ground. In that place a sacred gum-tree 'dreaming' rose up in the night. In another place he laid his spear on the ground. In that place he left a long cylindrical stone, another 'dreaming', undoubtedly a fertility site.

Also, when Eingana, the snake, the great fertility mother, came and lay on the vast empty plain of the earth, rolling about and moaning and filled with all forms of life, it was a spear which had to make the natural opening in Eingana before she could give birth.

As a weapon, the boomerang is unique to the Australian Aboriginals, although the ancient Egyptians are sometimes depicted using boomerang-like weapons with which to hunt birds in the swamps of the Nile delta.

The Aboriginals' boomerang, although widely used throughout the continent, was not known, or at least not used, for hunting and fighting in the far north-west, in north-eastern Arnhem Land, nor in the western half of South Australia.

There are three types of boomerang, the famous returning type, the non-returning type and the hook boomerang. All these were used for hunting and fighting. The boomerang is, of course, a throwing weapon. A true boomerang is made from timber with a natural curve of 'knee' in it. It is thus less likely to break on impact. It is a curved weapon with one side flat and the other slightly rounded. The rounded side is usually fluted in carved, parallel lines following its entire curve.

Many boomerangs are incised with tribal designs and motifs. It has been said that the designs and their actual execution on New South Wales and Queensland boomerangs are equal to those of any comparable work in the Pacific area. The long, slender boomerangs from the Lachlan-Darling Rivers district exhibit beautiful form and balance, and are covered with delicate tooling; since the colour of the mulga wood varies from cream to deep plum red, the mottled effect is most attractive.

The boomerang usually, but not always, tapers to a handgrip at its two ends. The Northern Territory boomerang has one handgrip end. Its creation is a simple but masterly example of aerodynamics. It is thrown with one end pointing in the direction of its flight, and must be made to spin continually in the air.

Alexander Vesper, an Aboriginal of a north coast tribe of New South Wales, gave me a 'dreamtime' tradition of the boomerang.

> A man who is now the green pigeon (his totem) made many boomerangs, both left-hand and right-hand boomerangs. While he was asleep a tribe came and stole them.
>
> Mamoogan, the boomerang maker, woke to find this tribe throwing his boomerangs about. He complained to the men that the boomerangs were his, but the men ignored him. They told him, 'These boomerangs are ours now.'
>
> Then Mamoogan began to mourn for his boomerangs. And as the men kept on throwing them, the boomerangs kept on flying out towards the sea. There they turned into swifts . . .

The same informant told me that the descendants of the Three Brothers, the first men to come to Australia, made boomerangs in imitation of the flights of swifts and swallows. They saw how it was possible to make a boomerang take to the air and return to the thrower. They also made non-returning boomerangs for fighting.

In a narrative given to me by Percy Mumbulla of Wallaga Lake on the south coast of New South Wales, a famous tribal elder called Merriman fights off an attacking tribe from his island in the lake. The boomerangs of Merriman were 'black and greasy, and even more power in them than his spears. They whined and whistled down on the attackers in their canoes, cutting off their arms and cutting off their heads. When those boomerangs hit the warriors they would cut through them and come flying back to Merriman.

'Merriman stood on his island catching his boomerangs out of the air with either hand, or picking them up from his feet and throwing them back again.'

A bark painting which was made for me at Port Keats, Northern Territory, and which is now in the possession of the New South Wales Art Gallery, is associated with an ancestral being who made the first boomerangs. The painting depicts boomerangs thrown by a fighting man, Wallagan, whose totemic form is a bird. The main design represents a boomerang-shaped mountain with streams leading down to the concentric circles, the totemic site.

In New South Wales at least, the returning boomerang had ritual and mythical significance. A narrative given to me by the Aboriginal Malcolm Rivers at Wallaga Lake tells of a tribal elder who made boomerangs.

He used to make boomerangs. He would call up a boy to go with him. He'd get his stone tomahawk and cut a circle in the ground. In this circle he'd put stringybark. Then he'd throw his boomerang and make it spin in the air over the bark. Up out of that stringybark smoke would start to rise. That stringybark would come alight. That's how this blackfellow could make fire.

He'd send that boomerang away. It would go far away and fall on the ground. He'd clap his hands and the boomerang would travel back to him along the ground.

This narrative is undoubtedly an example of a magico-religious practice concerned with the boomerang.

In an early photograph taken of a Bora initiation ceremony on the south coast of New South Wales, two lines of Aboriginals are holding boomerangs over a huge earth-formed figure of a man.

Once, in the Northern Territory, I was practising throwing the boomerang with a young Aboriginal. My companion was throwing it back to me for it was the non-returning type. The last time he returned it to me, it came spinning and curving back at a frightening pace. Passing well over my head, it shattered against a tree.

No doubt used less widely than the two boomerangs just discussed is the hooked boomerang. This weapon is similar in shape to the non-returning boomerang with the exception of its hooked end. It has one handgripping end and the curve in the weapon occurs closest towards its hooked end. The hook on the end projects back from the weapon's forward curve.

I have not seen this boomerang used either in fighting or hunting, but a tribesman at Port Keats demonstrated its use and explained it to me.

The weapon is thrown as are the other types—that is, the curved end points in the direction of flight—but with the difference that it is thrown to hit and bounce over the ground. The hooked end causes the bounding action. It is thrown to overtake and strike down a bounding kangaroo, a racing emu, or an adversary, and I would say that it would be an awkward and ugly weapon to avoid.

The Aboriginals' stone axe is an implement used hafted, or by gripping it in the hand. The blade of the stone is usually first flaked and then ground and polished smooth. Gripped in the hand, the rounded, smooth base of the head fits into the palm.

To make a haft for the axe, a suitable length of wood is heated in the middle. It is then bent round the middle of the head, the two lengths of the wood coming together to form the handle. The head is cemented in the loop of the handle with gum or resin and bound tightly with fibre or hair cord.

It was the stone axe, used by Aboriginals in climbing, which cut the notches in trees, seen in 1642 by Tasman's pilot, Visscher, in Tasmania. The distances between the notches caused Visscher to believe the country was inhabited by giants.

The following description of the Aboriginal method of climbing trees with a stone axe or tomahawk and a vine rope is by R. L. Dawson, who observed the practice by the Clarence and Richmond River Aboriginals of New South Wales some time after 1866.

Both on the Clarence and on the Richmond it was fascinating to watch the natives tree climbing with vine and tomahawk. As this method is now probably a lost art, it may be well to give a detailed description of it. Obtained from the brushes, the tough and pliable vine was usually about three-quarters of an inch in diameter and was cut to a length of fifteen to twenty feet. At one end a knot was tied forming a loop for the left hand. The vine was cast round the tree, the loop end being gripped by the left hand, while the right hand closed on the free end.

With tomahawk in belt, the climber was now ready to start. With slippery, smooth-barked trees it was necessary to cut shallow steps for the big toe all the way up, the first one or two being cut before leaving the ground. To cut subsequent steps, the climber, with left toe in a notch, brought the right hand end of the vine round under the right knee and then over the shin-bone and gripped it between the big toe and the next one. This gave a secure purchase and prevented the vine from slipping.

The right hand was thus released to grasp the tomahawk and cut two more notches, one to the right, and one to the left, and so on.

The climber ascended as a modern linesman with his belt round himself and a pole, moving the vine rope from notch to notch.

Should a possum or a bees nest be located about halfway up a hollow trunk, the Aboriginal cut fairly deep right and left notches. Descending to the ground, he tied his vine behind him in a knot that would not slip. Grasping it again with either hand he climbed back to the notches already cut. Placing his feet firmly in them, he carefully adjusted the knotted part of the vine on the upper part of his posterior, the outward thrust of his legs from the tree keeping him firm and steady and the vine taut.

Thus he was able to do without a hand hold and to use the tomahawk with both hands. I have seen an Aboriginal chop for half an hour in this position. They were so sinuous and deft in their movements, especially in the wristy and graceful play of the tomahawk, with never a blow misplaced, that it was a great pleasure to watch them. Mostly they climbed naked except for a belt for the tomahawk. Sometimes while resting or shifting position in a tree, they hooked this implement over the right shoulder and kept it in place by slightly elevating the shoulder and pressing downward with the cheek and jaw-bone.

Stone knives are used both as implements and weapons. They consist of a single flake of stone with a knob of gum attached for the handgrip. Central Australian stone knives are often curved; they are used for fighting, like a ripping tooth. A flake of stone can be set on the end of a digging stick and used as a carving tool.

The range of clubs to be wielded in the hand, or thrown, is wide and varied. They range from the heavy, straight stick, plain or often beautifully incised, to the boomerang-shaped, but hatchet-bladed 'lil lil' clubs of western New South Wales. The latter are also attractively incised. Other clubs are knobbed or pointed, and are also incised and painted.

One of the most deadly wooden weapons I have seen is a kind of broad-bladed wooden sword. I first saw this weapon in a camp at Beswick, Northern Territory. From memory, it was about one to one and a half metres long, a heavy, flat, broad-bladed weapon. Its handgrip ended in a fishtail shape. Later, at Port Keats, I was given a tradition which contained a significant reference to this weapon.

The tradition is from the Murinbata tribe, and the weapon, in that language, is called *leirwin*. It belongs to the great ancestral being, the Rainbow Snake, which accounts for its handgrip ending in a fishtail. In shape, the weapon could be compared to a symmetrical fish. Paintings of the Rainbow Snake often end in a fishtail. This ancestral being will be considered in another chapter.

'Kunmanngur (the Rainbow Snake) sat down in the ring of the old-men, called Bilambi. He used the long fighting and singing stick, the ironwood, spearblade-like, fork-tailed *leirwin*. He made, and gave those men their song. As Kunmanngur sang, the apostle bird man whirled the bullroarer on its hair-string.'

Thus it can be realised that Aboriginal weapons and implements have a sacred, or 'inside' significance as well as their common use and meaning. Perhaps it should be explained that, in the above extract, the Rainbow Snake used the *leirwin* as a sacred songstick. In other words, the sacred song inhabits the songstick.

Aboriginal fighting shields vary from the oval, concave wooden shields of Central Australia, and the long, oval shields of the northern part of the continent, to the narrow shields used in Victoria and New South Wales for parrying or deflecting spears and boomerangs. These shields are carved from a solid piece of timber with a carved handgrip behind the face of the shield. They are usually painted in striking representations of snakes, fish etc, or in motifs and designs.

The wooden coolamon used by the women for carrying water, holding gathered food, or even carrying an infant child, is a beautiful example of Aboriginal handcraft. Shaped like a boat and hollowed from a single piece of wood, it will float on the surface of a billabong to hold lily bulbs and mussels.

I have seen a shallower type of coolamon used by Western Australian Aboriginals for gathering grass seeds. It is called a *yandy*, and 'yandying' is the intricate, rhythmical moving, flipping and shaking of the vessel, held in the two hands, to separate the fine grass seeds from husks, grass fragments and sand in the dish.

Sometimes a coolamon is made from the large knobs or swellings which form on gum-trees, or is simply a piece of paperbark, bunched up at both ends and tied. An important implement for the women is the digging stick. This is simply a sharpened, stout stick used for digging out yams, honey ants, grubs and lizards.

It will be recalled that the ancestral beings, the Djankawau, the two sisters, used their yamsticks to make ritual wells or centres. Also, in a New South Wales myth, the seven sisters (the Pleiades) carried yamsticks, 'in the ends of which were inserted charms which protected the girls from their enemies'.

Dillybags and larger net bags are woven by the Aboriginal women with great skill and artistry. I have seen these made in the Northern Territory from pandanus palm fibre. The long palm leaves are gathered, the outer edges of thorns are stripped off, and the leaves torn or split into strands for weaving. The dillybag is closely woven. The ones in my possession have lasted for years and are still as good as when they were made.

The dillybag, carried by the women, is suspended by fig-bark cords from a woven forehead fillet, and hangs down over the wearer's back leaving the hands free.

The men's dillybag hangs in front from the neck, or is carried in the armpit. These are smaller bags containing the owner's personal belongings. They can also hold sacred possessions, such as stones or bones for magico-religious practices. In the quoted extract of the myth of the Old Man and the Six Namatoona, it was seen how the old man carried the sacred stone objects in his dillybag. Here the significance of the dillybag is the womb.

Rope for turtle and dugong spearing is made by the Aboriginals from coarser bark fibres, but I have also seen how the fine, strong, fig-bark cord is made.

At Milingimbi I was sitting with an old man in his camp. He had beside him a bundle of the rootlets that fig-trees or banyans let down from their boughs. The rootlets were cut into lengths of about twenty centimetres. As the old man was toothless, he handed one of the root lengths to his youngest wife, who was grinding lily seeds on a stone. The girl bit along the root and then peeled the skin off like bark. This she put in her mouth and began chewing as she carried on with her occupation of grinding the lily seeds.

After a while the old man's wife handed him an amount of chewed fibre. The old man teased and drew out a length of the fibre and rolled it on his thigh, twisting it. He joined another length to the first by rolling it on his thigh and twisting the two lengths together, continuing the process until he had a length of some two metres. He then rolled and twisted the whole length, holding one end with his left hand until, by doubling it, it twisted of its own tension into a single cord. The whole process took only a matter of minutes.

Canoes were made by the Aboriginals both from bark and from solid tree-trunks cut and hollowed out. In the account of the Three Brothers, the first Aboriginals to come to Australia, the brothers, after losing their ship in storm, wished to return to 'the central part of the world'.

They went up the Clarence River in New South Wales, and found a blackbutt tree (*Eucalyptus gigantea*). They stripped off the bark, made a big, long fire, and heated the bark until it was flexible. From this four- to five-metre sheet of bark they made a canoe. Three canoes were made by this method.

Canoes of this type were simply folded in two, the ends pierced and sewn together with vine or bark cord. The ends were sealed with gum and the sides kept apart by a stick wedged across the bows. These canoes were paddled by the occupant who knelt in the vessel and used a piece of bark in each hand. Such canoes used on lakes, lagoons and billabongs were shallow craft, their ends bunched together and tied. The occupant of these canoes stood upright and poled the crafts.

A canoe of a different order is the Northern Territory type cut and hollowed from a single tree. The Aboriginals learned to make these canoes from the Macassars who visited their shores. An axe or tomahawk of steel is required to cut and carve out such a canoe.

I once saw one of these canoes being made near a river mouth about eighty kilometres east of Darwin. It was being made by a Liverpool River tribesman who had obtained the loan of a tomahawk for helping a white man. We could hear the *thwock, thwock* of the tomahawk from our camp. My friend took me into the mangroves to see the canoe.

The craft was nearing completion. It lay as the tree, a milkwood, had been felled. At one end was the stump, at the other end the lopped-off head of the tree. The Aboriginal was working on the inside of the canoe as we came up. When he stopped and had a smoke with us, a girl from his camp carried on the work with the tomahawk. I ran my hand over the new, yellow, carved out wood. It was some six metres long, a creation of symmetry and balance. The curving sides were cut away to less than half a centimetre in thickness. Towards the bow a block was left to take the mast. I wanted to tell the tribesman that he was an artist, a sculptor, a poet, but could not find the words in his language to do so.

This canoe, like all these Macassar canoes, was an ocean-going one. It would be used with paddles and a sail, and would take the tribesman and his girl back to their 'country'.

I have also seen these canoes far up the Roper River. They are used far inland in the Northern Territory on the billabongs and lagoons. I used to lie in one and drift down the billabong covered with the white, starlike flowers that fall from the fig-trees.

5 Family and tribe

An Aboriginal tribe is an enlargement of the family circle. The enlarged family circle may be a number of groups or clans. In north-eastern Arnhem Land it was found that forty or fifty people belonged to a clan occupying a common territory which averaged 580 square kilometres.

The Wulumba tribe, which occupies an area from Cape Stewart to Blue Mud Bay in this region, is divided into a number of clans. These clans speak varying dialects of the Wulumba tongue.

The whole tribe is divided into two moieties. The moieties are exogamous. This means that the two groups are the basis on which marriage rules depend. The division of the people into two groups is said to have begun in the eternal Dreaming Period, when the Djanggawul ancestral beings gave birth to the first male and female predecessors of the present day groups. These two groups are known as *dua* and *jiritja*.

Dua and *jiritja* divide the whole life of the people and their known universe into the two groups and affiliates, all individuals belonging to one moiety. *Dua* appears to be associated with the Dreamtime belief, ritual and ceremony of the people, while *jiritja* is concerned with introduced or external themes. The Djanggawul and Wauwaluk ancestral beings, guardians of the most sacred ritual, are *dua*, while Macassan and Torres Straits mythology, ritual, songs and beliefs are *jiritja*.

Aboriginals are polygamous. An old man who was one of my informants at Milingimbi was reputed to have had twenty wives. There were at least six of his wives in the camp. Another of my informants had only one wife. In both these cases, and indeed in all Aboriginal tribes, marital partners are selected in accord with the rigidly defined social organisation and kin-relationship of the tribe.

Briefly, kin-relationship is based on the fact that a man calls his brother's children his sons and daughters, and they call him father, as they do their own father. A man's children and his brother's children call each other brothers and sisters. A woman regards her sister's children as her children, and she calls her sister's husband, husband.

A man calls his sister's children nephews and nieces, and they call him uncle, and his wife, aunt. A sister calls her brother's children nephews and nieces; they call her aunt and her husband, uncle. A man's sister's children call his children cousin.

These relationships are extended to distant members of the tribe, and individuals behave towards one another in accordance with their relationships. A man's wife must belong to a different group or clan and, in a tribe divided into two moieties, to the opposite moiety to himself.

An Aboriginal's wife is usually promised to him before she is born, or the infant girl is betrothed to the man through an arrangement with her parents' mother's brothers, mother's mother's brother, and wife's brother, with the consent of the elders of the group concerned. It is the duty of the man to whom the girl is betrothed to make presents of food to the parents of the child 'to grow her up'.

In cases of marriage between old men and young girls, the old men hold the view that the practice is beneficial to the girls and the young men. The girls should be married at puberty, but the boys should not be married before they have been disciplined. It is both a social and an economic arrangement, the motive cannot be said to be simply sexual. It provides an equitable balancing of marriage obligations, and is a security for the man in old age. If the old man already has a wife of similar age to himself, she does not question the arrangement. The old wife regards the matter in this light: 'Poor old man must have young wife to get honey and water for him.'

In the case of a young man who has been initiated in the Murinbata tribe, two brothers come to him six months after the initiation. They tell him to go and make his camp with the girl who has been given to him. They give the girl to him. The old men tell the girl that she must stay with this young man and inform her of the punishment if she does not obey.

Aboriginals are extremely fond of their children. Young boys are not corrected until they leave their parents' camp and go to the camp of the young men. At Milingimbi I saw a spoilt child sitting on the beach, crying and refusing to come to the camp of its parents. The parents did not scold it, but left the child to scream on the beach. The tide was coming in. When the water reached the child, it quickly decided that it wanted to be with its parents.

When boys are of age, the discipline meted out to them is very severe. They are disciplined by the tribal elders and made ready for their initiation rites into manhood. Two old men from Woodenbong in New South Wales recalled their discipline by the elders. They told me that, among other measures, a group of them were taken into the bush by the tribal elders. A bulldog-ants' nest was stirred up. One by one the old men signed to them to lie down on the nest. The ants ran all over them, biting them. The boys dared not disobey nor cry out. After a while, at a sign from one of the elders, the boys were told to get up from the nest. The ants were still running over them and biting them. The boys dared not move or attempt to brush the ants away.

'We were too frightened,' the men told me. 'Those old men had clubs and stone axes. They would have killed any boy who did not obey, or who cried out. After a while the old men took bushes and brushed the ants off us. In our day the young people had to do as the old men said. They would kill you if you didn't.'

The number of people in an Aboriginal tribe varies, but the findings of the anthropologist W. L. Warner, who did extensive field work in the region discussed at the beginning of this chapter, can be taken as a basis.

As nomadic hunters and food-gatherers, an Aboriginal clan or tribe moves and camps over the country in accordance with the seasons and the food supplies. When the yellow butterflies came to the northern end of the New England Range in New South Wales, the Aboriginals there knew that it was time, with other groups and tribes, to move up into what is now Queensland, to gather the nuts of the bunya pine.

In March the Aboriginals watched for the arrival of the blue mountain parrots in the mountain forests. If the birds were in flocks, they knew that there would be plentiful supplies of sea-mullet arriving in the bays along the sea coast during June. Or, as an Aboriginal friend of the Bunjalung tribe, New South Wales,

Aboriginal family at a mission in Arnhem
Land, NT.

Macassar-type canoe with mast and sail.
Melville Island is in the background.

A fairly typical Carpentarian Aboriginal. He is
wearing bands of bark fibre string with birds'
feathers twisted in them, used on Groote
Eylandt, NT.

An Aboriginal of Bathurst Island, NT, holding
a carved and painted figure of an ancestral
being or cult hero. These figures are often
sacred and used in ritual.

Housing at Yirrkala provided by the Missions of Welfare, NT.

An Aboriginal of Mornington Island, Gulf of Carpentaria (Lindsay Roughsey). In physique and body hair he resembles the physical types of Central Australia.

The intelligent face of a tribal elder on Groote Eylandt, NT.

informed me: 'In the winter time the tribes all along this coast used to camp in the hills and caves in the mountains, where there was plenty of firewood, and plenty of tucker, wallaby, porcupine, possum and all that. Summer time, they'd make down to the beaches for a feed of fish. They'd change their food.'

Being always on the move, the Aboriginals restrict their material possessions to the simplest essentials. Their shelters can be left behind and fresh ones made when the need arises. Walking one day with an Aranda tribesman in the desert, I noticed a large grinding-stone beside the track. I drew his attention to it. 'Oh yes,' he said, 'the old people left that behind.' It would be there when the people returned to that part of the country to gather and grind grass seed again.

An encampment is quite often simply a scattered group of windbreaks, each made from branches and bushes laid in a low semicircle against the prevailing wind. Inside the windbreaks there are fires around which the families sit or lie. Nine months of the year in the Northern Territory are ideal for lying under the stars.

In the summer, before and after the wet season, all that is desirable is a 'shade' of branches. This is simply a number of green branches propped against a tree to provide shade under which the family camps. During the prolonged wet season in Northern Australia, more substantial dwellings are made. One of these in eastern Arnhem Land, is called *leadamala*. It is a round or dome-shaped bark humpy with two opposite entrances and a hole in the top through which the smoke may escape. A smoking fire also provides relief from mosquitoes, which are troublesome in this region during the wet season.

Another type of shelter, which also helps to abate the mosquito problem is the 'pile house'. This is a bark house constructed on four forked posts about two and a half metres high. Bearers are placed in the forks to support the floor. Fires with more smoke than flame are made beneath the house. Forked sticks are used as ladders to climb up to this house.

Yet another shelter in this region in the wet season is one made from two- to three-metre sheets of stringybark. Two parallel trenches are dug and the ends of the sheets of bark are placed in them so that they form a symmetrical archway. Two or three sheets of bark are used, making a house of about two metres in length. One end of the house is closed with bark, the other end left open. The structure is covered with a heavy coating of paperbark. Sand, stones and logs are placed against the sides to keep the house firm in strong winds. These houses keep completely dry even in the heavy rains, which have to be experienced to be believed.

The desert Aboriginals make well constructed shelters. These are also dome-shaped. Fairly heavy curved boughs are embedded in the earth in a circle. The boughs curve over and meet or interlock to make the framework of the dome. The structure is thickly thatched with porcupine grass, or spinifex, or branches and bark. Outside, at the one entrance, one may see the gear of the camp, such as carrying vessels. Spears may be leant against the dwelling or stuck in the sand when a man is present. The personal dillybags of the women are kept inside the shelter.

These desert shelters are so well built that I have seen the framework still standing on station properties long after the 'old people', the tribal Aboriginals, have departed or died out. I saw these deserted frameworks between Beetoota in western Queensland and Tibooburra in New South Wales with the drift sand piled up against them.

Clothing, which we wear with conscious modesty to keep warm, or to protect us from the weather, is not so worn by the Aboriginals. From photographs and drawings we know that the Aboriginals of Tasmania and the southern parts of the mainland did wear wallaby and kangaroo-skin cloaks. This, no doubt, was for protection against prevailing cold weather. For the Aboriginals clothing is for personal adornment, or as a sign that a man has reached a certain stage of initiation. A girl may wear a fur tassel or pearl-shell pubic pendant as a sign that she has reached the age of marriage.

At Port Keats, the hair-belt, worn round the loins of a man, is the sign that he has reached his initiation stage. The young man is called *yunguana*. After his initiation the old men rub him over with charcoal and ashes and paint him with red ochre. They put a man's hair-belt on him and hang a bird's wing on it in front. They put a hair-band round his forehead and a wallaby-fur string band round his neck.

As my old friend Percy Mumbulla of the south coast of New South Wales said, 'Those old fellows went naked through the bush and never knew what sickness meant.'

Percy did tell me that his tribe possessed wallaby skin and possum skin rugs sewn up with kangaroo sinews. These rugs were called *bejahs*, and were unrolled when the tribal group made its camp.

Dick Donelly, a full-blood Aboriginal of the north coast of New South Wales, told me that he was born in a 'blady-grass' camp. His tribe wove their sleeping-mats from this blady-grass which, he said, was given to them by their god.

In one of the myths from this area a girl who is betrothed to a man follows, at about a day's walk behind him, the track to his country in the mountains at Woodenbong. She camps where he has camped the first night and carries a bundle of tea-tree bark for her blanket and her bed.

6 Ritual and mythology

Considered merely as 'theatre', an Aboriginal ritual
or corroboree can be as perfect a presentation as our
ballet, a production in which all the components of
ballet—music, décor, costumes, choreography,
dancing and mime, lighting and story—are fused in a
perfect art-form.

A cleared space in the bush is the stage, trees arching under the stars are the decor.
The dancers, painted and in costume, enter from the 'wings' of the bush. The
orchestra is the songmen, the *tjong tjong* sound and rhythm of the songsticks, the
booming and breathing rythm and timbre of the drone pipe or didgeridoo, the
clapping of hands, the boomerangs quivered together, the slapping of thighs.

The choreography, the composition of dancing, is traditional. The lighting is
the fire, between the dancers and the songmen, throwing the whole scene into
dramatic relief. The 'story' of the ritual is the myth, centuries old, which the
dancers re-enact and invoke.

Here the comparison with ballet must end because the nature of Aboriginal
ritual is religious and sacred. To seek a parallel in our society we should have to
enter a cathedral or church where a mass, or a high mass, is being held. There,
believers know that God, the great Ancestral Being, is present. The solemn rite,
performed by the priests in their vestments, invokes His mercy and benevolence.
From its sanctum on the altar, the Host, the 'body and spirit of our Lord', is
removed and shown to the hushed and reverent participants.

This recalls my meeting with the Aranda tribesman, Tonanga, better known as
Albert Namatjira, the painter. Tonanga took me about two miles away from the
camp and down into a sandy creekbed. Where a shade of branches leaned against
a ghost gum, a circle of old men were sitting in the sand. Tonanga introduced me
to the group and we sat down in the circle. After a while one old man went round
to the back of the shade. He returned with a cornsack which he placed in
Tonanga's lap. Out of the sack Tonanga drew a large, flat, black oval stone
inscribed on both sides with totemic designs. This stone was the Talkarra, the
body and spirit of Tonanga's ancestral being.

This object was viewed with great reverence by the circle of old men. Each man
reached forward in turn and placed the ball of his right thumb on the central
design of the stone while Tonanga explained the meaning and significance of the
Talkarra to me.

One old man then rubbed red ochre into the designs on the stone, placed it
inside the corn sack, and returned it to its hiding place. It was on this occasion
that Tonanga related to me the tradition of Erintja, the dingo ancestor. Tonanga
both related and acted the tradition, getting down on his hands and knees in the
sand. In some parts of the narrative he was corrected by the old men. A note by the
authority on Aranda traditions, T. G. H. Strehlow, is most relevant at this point.

All myths and traditions when told before a group of men are punctuated at frequent intervals by comments made by members of the audience. Expressions of agreement inform the story-teller that, in the opinion of his listeners, he is relating the tradition or the myth correctly. If he should omit some important detail, the others will remind him of it without delay: there is no such thing as a passive audience when myths or legends are being told in the hearing of a group of men, all of whom consider themselves to be guardians of the sacred traditions.

The Aboriginals had no written language. Their mythology is oral, and has been handed down through the centuries either in chanted form or in spoken narrative. A myth is often interspersed with songs or chants, which are the poetry of the narrative. 'In the old days,' an informant told me, 'the myths were never told without the songs.' There were narratives that would go on for night after night, in something of the manner of a serial story. The story would be told until everybody sitting round the fire became sleepy. The next night the story-teller would pick up the narrative from where he left off and continue it until everybody became sleepy. At dramatic or beautiful parts in the story, individuals in the audience would call out their appreciation.

These narratives and songs compare with the best in our literature. The narratives have artistic form, a beginning, middle and end. Their themes are beautifully developed and brought to dramatic and telling conclusions. The anthropologist R. M. Berndt has translated in the appropriate verse form the song-cycles of the Djanggawul and Kunapipi myths and cults. T. G. H. Strehlow has translated, together with their musical notations, the poetry, the songs and chants of the Aranda.

The meaning and significance of ritual is to ensure the continuation of the species in all forms of life, and to ensure the fertility and productive qualities of the earth. To the Aboriginals, social organisation and law, which came from their ancestral beings, are stressed in their mythology and ensured in their ritual.

In the following extract from a tradition of an ancestral being, the Rainbow Snake, from the Murinbata tribe at Port Keats, there is an explanation of the significance of baptism.

At the river the Rainbow Snake cut and made a long, hollow bamboo. He filled this bamboo with flying-fox men. He blocked the end and put the bamboo down into the water. He filled up another bamboo with flying-fox men and put that down into the water. The fishing net, *kullai*, which the Rainbow Snake made the first time, he filled also with flying-fox men and put in the water. He kept the flying foxes under the water all day.

The Rainbow Snake stood right up out of the water on his nails near his tail and looked all around. Now all the trees stood up and all the trees were in flower. He called out the names of the trees: *kunmurrin* the gum-tree with red flowers, *pirroo* the gum-tree with white flowers. *Werr*, the paperbark tree, stood up. They flowered with white flowers and the Rainbow Snake gave them their name.

And the Rainbow Snake stood up in the water and looked out more trees for the flying foxes in the bamboos. And the trees rose up everywhere. Out of *maluk*, the bamboo, the Rainbow Snake let the flying foxes stream up into the flowering trees. And out of the fishing net, *kullai*, he let them stream. He called out to them, 'I let you go now. No matter how far you want to go to look for food, you can go. Come back before daylight. All night you can feed. You do not sleep.' 'Yes father,' all the flying foxes called back.

Always now the Rainbow Snake puts the bamboo to his mouth and blows out the spirits of the flying foxes. As he blows, he makes a spray of water and the rainbow curves over his head. And the bands of the rainbow are the spirits of the flying foxes blown out of the bamboo of the Rainbow Snake.

In this extract of the Aboriginal creation time, called *kardoorair*, which means, 'At first all forms of life were men' the creator returns the men of the flying-fox totems to the water, the primal source of all life. The hollow bamboo, in which they are contained, is the ritual drone-pipe, called *maluk*. Its significance in this case is the womb. The fishing net has a similar meaning. The creator stands up out of the water, the source of life, and the flowering trees spring up. The Rainbow Snake releases the flying-fox men, reborn in their totemic forms, to stream into the flowering trees. One might well put the words that God used of Jesus at His baptism into the mouth of the Aboriginal creator, 'These are my beloved sons, in whom I am well pleased.'

The same concept is expressed in the myth of Eingana from the Djauan tribe on the Roper River. 'That first time, creation-time, we call Biengana. The first being we call Eingana. We call Eingana our mother. Eingana made everything. Eingana had everything inside herself that first time.

'Eingana is snake. She swallowed all the blackfellows. She took them, inside herself, down under the water. Eingana came out. She was big with everything inside her. She came out of the big water-hole near Bamboo Creek. Eingana was rolling about, every way, on the ground. She was groaning and calling out. She was making a big noise with all the blackfellows, everything, inside her belly.'

Eingana gave birth to all the forms of life. She is the source of all life, of the spirit in all its totemic forms. This is the very heart of Aboriginal religious belief. This concept of Eingana as the inexhaustible source of life and spirit shows that in Aboriginal thought, birth, death and re-birth recur in continuous cycles. It is also an expression of Aboriginal totemism, that is, that spirit is common to all forms of life, and indeed, to all that is in the earth and the universe.

The myth continues: 'No one can see Eingana. In the raintime, when the flood water comes, Eingana stands up out of the middle of the floodwater. She looks out at the country. She lets go all the birds, snakes, animals, children belonging to us . . .'

These are the fundamental explanations of the significance of baptism. Until a child has been baptised, it has not been spiritually born. Just as there is ritual in Christian baptism, so is there elaborate ritual in spiritual birth among the Aboriginals.

In initiation rites such as *kunapipi* in the north, in which initiates are circumcised, or rites in the south where tooth evulsion was practised, the significance of these acts could be expressed as the release of the spirit. Such an initiate must remain for a period in an 'unborn' state. A young man in this state, and his emergence from it was described and explained to me by an old man of the Murinbata tribe.

After the young man, *yunguana*, has been out in the bush for three months with the old men, an old man brings him back to the circle of old men called *bilambi*. The *yunguana* sits in the centre. The old men sing him, they cut the vein in their forearms and put the blood in a paperbark coolamon. They rub the man all over with their blood. They give him their blood, congealed, to swallow.

The *yunguana* must crawl through the straddled legs of the old men to the

camp. The women cut their heads and cry. They are sorry for that young
man who has been away so long.

The *yunguana* comes back to the old men because he has been fed with
their blood. This bull-roarer, that comes from the Rainbow Snake, is
whirled round the head of the young man. We show this bull-roarer to the
young man.

After the initiate has washed himself in the creek he is ritually adorned (as
previously described) by the old men. He is taken back to the camp and his
mother gives him food. He can now eat the food of the camp. The old man tells
him that he can now speak. For six months the mother feeds the young man. The
young man hunts wallabies and brings them back to his mother.

This extract explains how the initiate is spiritually in an embryonic state. He is
segregated in the bush under a ban of silence. The motherlike behaviour of the
old men is demonstrated as they feed him with their own blood as a mother's
blood feeds her unborn child. Crawling through the straddled legs of the old men
is an act of birth.

The assumption of the ritual of spiritual birth has been mentioned in the myth
of the two ancestral beings, the Djankawau. It will be recalled that men stole the
dillybags containing *rangga* of ritual from the two sisters. When the sisters found
their dillybags gone, they heard the sound of the ritual the men were making.
They covered their ears and said, 'Now we cannot hear this ritual. It belongs to
the men.'

If it is thought that this eating or drinking of human blood, in ritual, is
barbarous, then we should remember that our own rite of Communion, refined
through the centuries, of tasting the wine and eating the wafer, means that the
Son of God is present saying, 'This is my body, and my blood.'

Briefly stated, this first initiation is the beginning of 'rites of passage' which
grade an Aboriginal through his life from youth to old age. Such rites as *lorrkun*,
ngalmark, *kunapipi*, *yaburdurawa* and *marraian* mark the stages of his
advancement, and it is not until he has grey hairs that the final revelations of his
tribe's rituals and totemic emblems are imparted and revealed to him.

Women, to an exoteric or 'outside' degree, take part in the rituals of the men.
The 'inside' part of the men's rites, and the emblems associated with them, are
strictly forbidden to women. If a woman should see anything associated with the
sacred nature of these rites, even by accident, she would be killed by the men.
Women have secret myths and ritual dances of their own. They, in turn, will not
reveal anything of their secret religious life to the men.

The sacred nature of ritual and the severe exclusion of women from the men's
knowledge are illustrated by the account of Narpajin, the daughter of the
Rainbow Snake, which was given to me by an informant of the Murinbata tribe.

Two old women went out looking for food. A big wind came up and blew
towards them. On the wind they heard the sound of singing, and they heard
the sound of a songstick, *tjong-tjong*. The two women stopped and listened.
Then one old woman became frightened. 'Oh, come on,' she said. 'You and I
must run away.' They put their hands over their ears and ran away. A long
way off they stopped and sat down. Still that song came down to them on the
wind. 'Oh,' said the first old woman, 'we two have heard something.' 'What
something?' said the other. 'Oh, a song something. Some devil is there,' the
first old woman wailed.

The old man Padorooch came up. 'Old man, we have heard something,'
the old women called. 'What did you hear?' asked the old man. The women

began to sing the song they had heard on the wind. The old man Padorooch
hissed at them. He put his hands over their mouths. 'Where did you hear
this? Come on, you two, show me,' the old man said.

The wind had stopped blowing. The two women took the old man close
up to the place from where the sound of the singing had come. 'Did you see
anything?' asked the old man. 'No,' said the two women, 'we were too
frightened.' 'All right,' said the old man. He took the two women back to the
camp.

Padorooch called up the old men. The old men sat down in a ring.
Padorooch spoke. 'Bye and bye those two women will tell everyone about
that song. We must kill them.' The old men killed those two women.

Now the old man Padorooch tied himself up all over in paperbark. He
made two slits in the paperbark for his eyes. He went back to the place of the
singing. The wind was blowing again. The old man heard a song coming
down on the wind. 'Ah,' he said, 'that song is Nunjeeboin, the sacred song,
all right.'

The old man sneaked up and sneaked up. Then, coming down on the
wind, he heard another song. 'Ah, that is Krungarra, that is another "inside"
song.' The old man sneaked up. The singing led him up to the big rock-hole
Oolai. The old man sneaked up on his knees. He crouched down. Through
the slits of the paperbark he saw the Rainbow Snake, Narpajin. She was half
woman and half snake. Down to the waist, she was woman. From the waist
down, she was snake. She was sitting down, coiled up. She was hitting the
songstick, and singing.

As the old man crouched down, a big kangaroo came up to the water-hole
to drink. As Narpajin sat singing she watched the kangaroo. She killed the
kangaroo with her eye. The old man did not move. 'Hah,' he thought, 'I will
stay here all day. I must watch and listen.'

As Padorooch crouched there he saw the Rainbow Snake making the bull-
roarer Ngowaroo with a stone-knife. She cut the bull-roarer with the design
of the kangaroo dreaming, the palm-tree dreaming, and the yam dreaming.
She cut the bull-roarer with the design of the road of Narpajin, joining up
the dreaming places, the totemic sites.

When the old man had seen this, he drew back and back. He sneaked away.
He went back to the camp and called up all the old men. He gave them the
song, the law, and made the Ngowaroo of the Rainbow Snake.

The old man said that he must go back to the waterhole of Narpajin. 'You
old men had better tie me up in paperbark,' he said. 'And paint all over the
paperbark with mud so that the snake cannot smell me,' he added.

A big wind was blowing when the old man heard the singing again
coming from a long way off. The old man sneaked up, and sneaked up to the
waterhole. He saw the snake-woman sitting on the bank with half the snake
end of her body in the water. She was sitting and singing with her back to the
old man, and beside her and a little bit behind her was a round, flat stone
covered with markings. 'Hah! That is a good stone, I must steal it,' thought
the old man.

He got a hooked stick. He sneaked up close to the snake-woman. He
slowly reached out with the stick and slowly drew the stone away. The old
man did not touch the stone with his hand. He drew it back with the stick for
a long way. He sat down and looked at the stone.

'Ah, I cannot touch this stone,' thought the old man. He drew the stone
over to an ant-bed. The ants ran out and, as they ran over the stone, the stone

killed them. 'Ah,' said the old man to himself, 'this stone is from the belly of Narpajin. This stone is poison. It is better that I leave this stone for a long time for the rain and the wind and the sun to clean and dry it.'

Year after year the old man came back to look at that stone. 'Ah,' he said each time he came, 'this stone still has poison.'

At last the old man came and found the stone washed clean by the rains. The old man said to himself, 'It might be that this stone is called Larnja. It might be that it belongs to the Karwadi bull-roarer. It might be that the snake has some word about it. I will have to go back and listen again.'

The old man went back. He sneaked up to the water-hole. The Rainbow Snake was sitting down with sacred bull-roarers of many different rituals in front of her. She was talking to herself. She stood the bull-roarer Ngowaroo up against the bull-roarer Karwadi. She said, 'This one is Ngowaroo, this one Kunapipi, this one Pargolah, and this one is Kurraba. All these belong to Karwadi, and Karwadi belongs to the Murinbata men. And this one Tjubbun belongs to Karwadi. Ah, where is that Larnja, the spirit-stone from my belly, the mother of all these?'

And there the old man Padorooch saw the bull-roarer of *Walam bootjoo bootjoo*, the Lightning Brother. 'Ah,' said the old man, 'that is my dreaming. That one is my spirit. I want to make that one.'

The old man went back and cut wood from the ironwood tree and made the Lightning Brother. He made all the bull-roarers he had seen. And he gave the rituals and laws of the bull-roarers Kunapipi, Pargolah, and Kurraba to the Djamunjun tribe, and the bull-roarers Karwadi and Ngowaroo he gave to the Murinbata tribe.

The rituals mentioned in this account, together with their bull-roarers or sacred ceremonial object, and also myths or cults previously mentioned in this chapter, as well as being performed for their initiating and age-grading significance are performed for their increase and fertility potency. Thus, after Kunapipi has been performed, food sources or game are abundant, and the Aboriginals will know that they sang and danced their ritual with potent effectiveness.

Magico-religious practices, usually performed by individuals or groups, are also rites. These practices are employed to attract a girl to a man who desires her, or vice versa, to mete out punishment to violators of tribal law, or for rain-making.

One of these love-magic rites was related and explained to me by a man of the Aranda-Luritja tribes in Central Australia. 'If a man wants a girl, he goes to an old man and tells him. The old man "sings" the girl for him. The girl then sees that the man who wants her looks different. She comes up to the man's camp and says, "I want you. I camp here tonight."

'The old man who can sing this song uses a small shining shell with a hole in it. He hangs this shell round his neck when he sings the girl.'

The myth that explains this practice, given to me by the same informant, is as follows.

The old man Tullapinja sits down at Gilbert Spring, which we call Thalaldooma. To make Gilbert Spring he opened the vein in his arm, *mullatjeeta*. This is dreaming (creation). Tullapinja looks up towards the east. He sees another old man sitting along Alice Creek, which we call Najatoonama.

Another time, old man Tullapinja should open the vein in his arm, but he

An Aboriginal playing the didgeridoo on a beach at Yirrkala, Arnhem Land, NT. The tone range of these instruments is amazing.

An Aboriginal songman, who sings the oral part of the ritual. His singing calls the dancers. Here the songman is using two boomerangs which he clashes and quivers together, marking the time and rhythm of the song. He also uses two songsticks which are sacred, for they contain the epic song cycles of the ritual and cult.

Preparation for a corroboree takes half a day or more, and corroborees are usually held at night. Here an old warrior of Derby, WA, makes himself up for the evening dance.

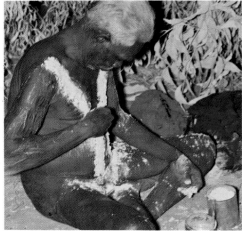

A Western Australian Aboriginal at work preparing the sacred symbols to be used in a forthcoming ritual.

Preparation for a corroboree on Mornington Island, Gulf of Carpentaria.

Decorated dancer performing during a sacred ritual with the didgeridoo or drone-pipe on Mornington Island, Gulf of Carpentaria. Smoke from fires surrounds corroboree scenes. Note eucalyptus leaves tied to the dancer's knees.

A line of dancers in the relaxed loping walk which intersperses each dance, in a ritual on Mornington Island.

opens the vein, *oolta*, in his side. All the blood runs out. He sees everything dark. He nearly dies. His eyes turn up and he sees a sky like clouds with water falling out of them.

Tullapinja sings then to make himself all right. He sings and puts up a big rainbow. There are a lot of women at Gilbert Spring. Tullapinja wants to show off to these women.

Old man Tullapinja sees another old man, Wainda the possum, in another place Warkulba. Old possum man says, 'Oh, that's old Tullapinja there. I can see him. I have nothing here. I am only here by myself. Old Tullapinja there has a lot of women.

Tullapinja looks out and says, 'Oh, there is another big lot of women along Kurralda.' Old Tullapinja turns to half a moon so those women can see him. Those women look out and say, 'Oh, big shining over there! I think we had better go.' Old Tullapinja whirls his *namatoona* [bull-roarer] and makes a noise like thunder, and makes lightning.

Old Tullapinja calls up all those women to Gilbert Spring. All those women are there. They are the pigeon women, Dorada, Pulkarra and Coo-coo-ka. *Co-coo-coo*, they talk, like that, that's those women. Old man Tullapinja has all those women and he goes down into that spring. He puts his head up like this. His head shows out of the spring. He puts a rainbow all round that place where the women are. All those women belong to him. They are all that old-man's wives.

Tullapinja keeps the women there while he goes walkabout and hunting for meat for those women. There is plenty of tucker for women in that place, *yalka*, the little yam, *tjurrka*, the wild fig, and *errwutta*, the little wallaby.

Old Tullapinja all the time turns moon, he turns rainbow. Mist and fog come all over that place. If Tullapinja hears some man coming, he puts out fog or mist to stop that man. That man can't see. Old Tullapinja makes rainbow, or turns into a moon.

Some women belonging to Tullapinja went out hunting. A man from the north saw those women and took them all away. Old man Tullapinja had gone to Amulda Spring. He sat down. He thought, 'Oh, I feel funny.' He went back to Gilbert Spring. He saw that only a few women were left there. He sent for the half moon, Tjerbookulka. The half moon turned into a man, and Tullapinja gave him a shield and a boomerang.

Tjerbookulka the half moon turned into an old man with a long white beard. When the sun went down he went north over the ranges to the place Elbakurdukka, where he found the man from the north with all those women. Tjerbookulka knelt down. He took his shield and boomerang and held them in the crooks of his arms, behind his back. He moved from side to side, and sang, and went down into the ground. He took all those women down into the ground with him. He left one old woman behind for the man from the north.

Tjerbookulka took all those young girls back to Gilbert Spring. There he turned back into the half moon again.

When a man wants a girl he sits down and sings this story. He sings the girl this story called Ilbinja. No young man can hear this story, only big married man. That man sings Tullapinja the old man, he sings Tjerbookulka the half moon, he sings Boolara the rainbow.

One day, when there is no cloud in the sky, the girl that man is singing sees lightning in the sky. She says, 'Oh, that lightning is close up.' Next day the lightning comes closer. That night she sees the man who has been singing

Opposite
Two pictures of the same corroboree—Aboriginals with a didgeridoo on Mornington Island, Qld.

her. She goes along to his camp. Only that one girl can see the lightning. That lightning shows up the man, and the girl comes to him and camps.

When a man sings Ilbinja, old Tullapinja makes that man different. The girl sees the man and likes him. She starts dancing. She shows off so that the man can see her. One girl that a man sang had a baby. It was a boy. That boy was my father. My father's name was Mulbunga, the scrub wallaby.

My brother wanted to get one of those shells. He went to Gilbert Spring. He saw all those shells in the water. But all those shells went down into the spring because they belong to Tullapinja.

One hesitates to comment on this myth because of its inherent poetry and mystery. It is evident that Tullapinja is an ancestral being of fertility. His behaviour is similar to that of the Rainbow Snake ancestor in the north.

A magico-religious practice, in this case from the Djauan tribe on the Roper River, used to punish or avenge violators of tribal law and social organisation, is described in the following account.

A man had run away with a *lubra* belonging to an old man. The man and the woman had run away together. The old man looked about for their tracks. He could find nothing. The man and the woman had travelled over the rocks. The old man looked about, looked about for their tracks. The old man cried, cried, cried. He looked all about the rocks, he looked along the river, all round the spring. He could find no tracks. The old man went back to his camp.

The old man gathered grass. He made string. He began to bind and tie up the grass until he had made a figure of a man. As the old man made this grass figure, he sang the man and woman who had run away from him. As he sang he fixed a stone axe on the shoulder of the grass figure. He fixed a stone axe on the other shoulder. He put a stone axe at one elbow, and he put a stone axe at the other elbow. After that, he put a stone axe at one knee, and he put a stone axe at the other knee. Like that the old man made Marrgon the lightning.

The old man sang the lightning. He sent the song, Yarrada, after those two who had run away. Bye and bye that old man sat down. He slept. He dreamed. He dreamed of those two who had run away.

The lightning followed up the man and the woman. The lightning followed them, followed them, followed them. Half way the lightning camped. He got up and went on again. He followed them, followed them.

The man and the woman had been out hunting. The man had killed a kangaroo. He had roasted the kangaroo. The lightning sneaked up, sneaked up, sneaked up. From a long way off the lightning smelled the grass where the man and the woman were cooking the kangaroo. Quick fellow, quick fellow, he sneaked up. He looked out for that man and woman. He found that man and woman.

The man looked back from where he was cooking the kangaroo. He looked. He saw an old man with white hair. 'Oh,' said the man to the woman, 'an old man has come up.'

The lightning had made talk-talk all the way, 'Boi, boi, boi, boi!' The lightning came up tall, all the same as this one tree. 'Spssh, spssh! Rai-rai-rai-dee-dee. Siss-siss-siss-siss!' He bled them. He split them up, finished them up. He went up along the sky.

That old man was asleep. He dreamed about the man and the woman. The lightning came back. The lightning had brought back to the old man the livers and hearts of the man and woman. The lightning showed them to the old man. Bye and bye the old man talked, 'O, you have killed them.' That old man was dreaming, you know.

Bye and bye the old man went away to another place. The old man travelled, travelled, travelled. The old man found the place where Marrgon the lightning had cut up his woman and the man who had run away with her.

No matter if it is a long way off that anyone sits down, that lightning will find them. Lightning, he is all bone. 'Rai-rai, dee-dee, Siss-siss,' he talks as he strikes, cuts anyone up.

Ngamul, he is different. He has stone spear, long one. He goes like fire, like star, when he runs, not little bit star, more big. He has white body, white painted body.

Magico-religious practices are many and varied, both for killing a victim and for healing anyone. On the coast of New South Wales, tribal avengers or executioners are known as *Doowan* or *ngaloongirr*. The *Doowan* are two men. Before they set out in pursuit of an offender, they stand in a circle of the old men. 'They stand face to face, foot touching foot. There comes a rush of wind like wings passing. Those two men are gone. They travel like the wind, like a rush of wings. They rush through the air. You hear stones rattle across the roof, that is the *Doowan*.'

The victim cannot escape the *Doowan*. Finally, the *Doowan* throw their *guneena*, which are magico-religious stones, at the victim, and in three days the offender dies.

Such executioners as the *ngaloongirr*, can, according to native belief, remove a victim's kidneys and fat, and close the wound while the victim is in a trance. The inflicted man awakes and pursues his normal activities but dies within three days.

If a victim has had a bone or a piece of quartz inserted in him by a *ngaloongirr*, a tribal doctor can use a magico-religious practice to remove the malignant object from the victim and cure him.

To the Aboriginals, fire, like all the elements, is spirit. In the myth of the two Wauwaluk sisters, the sisters made fire with the sacred *rangga* object. In a myth from the Roper River, a hero stole two firesticks from a man who afterwards became the crocodile. The hero, after giving the firesticks to the old man of the tribe, became the rainbow-bird, the bee-eater (*Merops ornatus*). This bird has two spine-feathers, the two firesticks, sticking out from his tail.

When the old man was given the two firesticks, he called the tribesmen out on to a plain and showed them the two sticks. Before this happened the tribesmen had no fire. One of these sticks had a hole and a notch made in its side in the middle. The other stick was sharpened slightly at one end.

The old man sat down and held the holed and notched stick with his feet over a little pile of shredded bark. Then he took the other stick between the palms of his hands and twirled it rapidly backwards and forwards with its sharpened end in the hole of the notched stick. After a while, the hole where the stick was twirling began to smoke. Out of the notch ran a little stream of burning wood dust which fell on to the shredded bark and set it alight.

This is the method of fire-making which I have seen used by Aboriginals of the Djauan tribe on the Roper River.

When a group of Aboriginals are travelling, a firestick is often carried. The stick is waved about now and then to keep its glowing end alight.

A rain-making practice, and the myth which informs it, was related to me by a man of the Ngeamba tribe of south-western New South Wales. A summary of this account is as follows.

The rain-maker is called a *wirreengun*. 'The rain-makers made the Rain-stone.' This is usually a piece of quartz-crystal. The rain-maker puts the rain-stone in a fork of a tree. My informant said that this stone affected 'the lightning like a battery'. To make the rain, the rain-maker's spirit has to travel up into the sky where the skins (water-skins) of the 'Everlasting Water' are guarded by a man with two huge savage dogs.

At night, the rain-maker sings the camp so that the people will not hear his spirit as it goes up into the sky. The rain-maker goes past the moon-man, who is sitting in his *mia-mia*. He goes past a 'creek of white water up there' until he comes to the sky-country where the skins of Everlasting Water are guarded by the man with two dogs.

When this man sees the rain-maker, he and his dogs rush to attack him. But the rain-maker directs his assailants' attention to two emus out on the plain of the sky country and the man and his dogs rush off after the emus.

While the man and the two dogs are away after the emus, the rain-maker starts slitting the water-skins with his rain-stone. The water pours out and through a prickly bush which purifies it. The man and his dogs rush back, but the rain-maker's spirit has got into the water and the dogs cannot bite him.

When the rain-maker returns to the earth, he sings a song to make the north wind blow and bring the rain. Or he sings another song if he wants the wind to come from the east and bring the rain.

If the rain-maker has a son, he takes his child with him on his back when he goes up into the sky-country to slit the water-skins. He takes his son with him while he is asleep. 'The rain-maker's power sort of grows in his son.' When his son grows up he becomes a rain-maker.

The myth behind this practice and belief has its origin in the Dreamtime, in the beginning. Men used then to live round a big swamp or lagoon. They lived off the gum of the yarran trees. The water in the swamp could never dry up. It was the Everlasting Water. The men held a meeting at this swamp to decide whether they should die and remain dead, or whether they should die and come back to life again. Everyone, with the exception of the man whose totem was the moon, decided that when they died they would remain dead. After the meeting all the men went out to gather the gum from the yarran trees.

While they were away, the eagle man came and filled up all the water-skins (water containers made from the skins of kangaroos) with the water in the swamp. He then flew up into the sky with the water-skins. When the men returned and found that there was only mud and slush left in the swamp, they changed into their totemic forms of the brolga, the plain turkey, the emu, the native cat, the red kangaroo and the black kangaroo, the bat, and the moon-man became the moon.

This is why the rain-maker now has to go up into the sky-country to burst the water-skins and get the Everlasting Water for the tribe.

The last of the 'rites of passage' for an Aboriginal are those which follow his death. These rites cover a period of many months and are performed to ensure that the soul of the individual is safely transferred from the physical and profane world to its spiritual and sacred source.

Taking the practice used in north-eastern Arnhem Land as an example, the corpse is ritually interred in the earth. In some cases it is given platform, or tree burial, the body being placed on a platform in a tree. After a period of three months, the body is exhumed, or taken down from its platform.

Relatives of the deceased clean the bones of the decayed flesh. The bones are then placed on paperbark and tied up in a bundle, and put in the fork of a tree near the camp. One man, the keeper of the bones, watches them for two or three months. At the end of this time he is told to bring them into the camp. They are placed in a cylinder of bark painted with the dead man's totemic emblems. The women take the cylinder and place it on two forked sticks near the camp. The mother of the deceased then takes the bones and carries them about with her for two or three months.

Eventually the bones, broken up with a stone, are placed in a hollow log which has been made from a hollow tree cut down, prepared and carved. Sometimes a bark or branch house is made for the log coffin. The coffin is again set up on two forked sticks until the log rots away.

A man's or woman's bones are sent back to their own 'country', and close to the totemic site of his or her spiritual emergence into the world. When the people are burning the grass in the dry season while hunting, the coffin and the bones may be burned and will go into the ground of their own country.

The whole of this practice is accompanied by rites of singing and dancing that satisfy the living as well as the dead that the soul, purified, has returned to its source, the totemic well or other site.

Cave burial was earlier known in this region. At the conclusion of the Waugeluk myth of this area, the Rainbow Snake ancestor, after giving the people the ceremonies of the hollow log interment, said, 'It is close up daylight now. I go into my cave. I have given you these ceremonies.' He went into a big cave and closed up the entrance with a big stone so that he could not come out.

7 Traditional and transitional art

A sacred painting which a Murinbata tribesman
made for me at Port Keats depicts a mountain top
where the great ancestral being, the Rainbow Snake,
lies in a huge coil. In this place the sacred ritual
objects of the tribe are hidden in the rock clefts. This
is the place where the Rainbow Snake gave the
Murinbata tribe their laws, ritual songs and dances,
and their painting.

In the myth of Eingana, the primal fertility mother, from the Djauan tribe on the Roper River, a hero called Barraiya had to spear the great snake as she writhed and moaned in birth travail. He made the spear wound, which was the natural opening that enabled Eingana to give birth. The hero then went back to his totemic site. There he painted himself on a rock and assumed the totemic form of the blue-winged kookaburra.

Similarly, the Wandjina, the creative beings of the northern Kimberleys, eventually went to various caves and rock shelters and became paintings. Their spirits remain in their paintings. Their spiritual power is available to the Aboriginals through the performance of ritual.

These examples demonstrate the nature of the sacred paintings of the Aboriginals. The first instance shows the authority of such paintings, as part of ritual and law. This authority is as sacred as the voice of God, who gave Moses the ten commandments on Mount Sinai.

Such Aboriginal painting is traditional. It is fixed, and not altered. An Aboriginal man inherits his totemic designs as he does his totemic myth, and the myths do not change. They are word for word as they were given out by the ancestral beings.

A sacred painting is charged with the same spiritual potency as a stone *tjurunga*, or *talkarra*, which is the body and spirit of the ancestral being in the same sense that we believe that the Host is the body and spirit of Our Lord.

Basic examples of Aboriginal art could be listed as follows:
Cave and rock paintings and rock engravings executed by ancestral beings
Paintings and carvings or incisions on ceremonial objects
Decorated ceremonial objects
Ceremonial ground paintings
Ceremonial body paintings
Wood and tree carvings
Bark paintings

These examples of Aboriginal art are integral to the pattern of religion, law, traditions and ceremonies which govern the Aboriginals' whole behaviour and existence.

There are two main types of Aboriginal art. One is the representational or 'X-ray' painting of northern Australia. The other type might be called the art of motifs and symbols. This type of art is primarily the practice of Central Australian tribes. Motif and symbol will be found in representational art but, as an example, Aranda art, Central Australia, is purely motif and symbol.

Paintings in caves and rock-shelters are known throughout the continent, including Tasmania. In Arnhem Land and on Groote Eylandt there are caves with ceilings of up to thirty metres long and from six to fifteen metres wide that are covered with paintings. In many cases the paintings are superimposed. This area of the continent is probably the richest in rock paintings, both for their abundance and artistic execution.

The paintings are in the usual earth colours available to the Aboriginals, that is, in red ochre and yellow orchre, white pipeclay and charcoal. Pigments of brown, purple and blue have also been recorded, and human blood was occasionally used.

Indonesian and Malaysian influences have enriched much of this art. In addition to animals, birds, fish, reptiles, and human figures, the Macassan *prau* appears superimposed on the earlier paintings. Contacts with later and modern times are also recorded in paintings of figures of Japanese pearlers, missionaries, water-buffaloes, luggers, ships and planes.

Some Aboriginal paintings have been made famous through modern book production. One such group is the Wandjina and Rainbow Serpent paintings of the Kimberleys of north-western Australia. Sir George Grey discovered these in 1838 when, in the Glenelg River district, he found the huge, dramatic and colourful figures staring at him from the cave walls. Wandjina figures are painted in various caves in this region. At Walcott Inlet, northern Kimberley, there is, among other figures, a Wandjina nearly five metres high. Another Wandjina is a single huge figure painted on a natural stone column.

The Wandjina are ancestral beings associated with the Rainbow Serpent and are concerned with the perpetuation of the seasons, with bringing rain, and are the source of spirit-children. Their myth is that they came from the wind, wandering across the country and creating its physiographical features. Finally, they went to various caves and became paintings.

Another famous group is the Lightning Brothers at Delamere in the Northern Territory. Reference to these beings has been made previously in an extract from an account from Port Keats. The Lightning Brothers are also associated with rain-making. The whole site of their location is a sacred rain totem. In their myth the two brothers were responsible for introducing the rite of sub-incision to the people of the Wadaman tribal country.

Stencilling was one of the earliest practices in cave painting in Australia. Examples of the stencilled human hand are well known. In the Worara tribe, northern Kimberleys, the hand stencil is a link between the living people and the spirit world. The Djauan tribe of southern Arnhem Land believes that it represents the deceased person and mourn over it in the same way.

In a myth told to me in south-western New South Wales, two sisters, who lived when there were no men in the world, made their home in a cave at Mount Manara. The inside of this cave is covered with stencilled human hands. One of these sisters conceived a child from a flower. The narrator told me that her son was like Jesus. He became a wise and clever man, and he came into the world without a father.

Stencils are also made from the feet of animals, birds and reptiles, from shield, boomerang, club and spear-thrower, with emu's head and neck. To make a stencil, the artist fills his mouth with a mixture of ochre and water, or pipeclay and water. He places his hand or the object against the rock-face, and then sprays the pigment with his mouth and lips over and round the hand or object. When the hand is removed, the silhouette or stencil is left on the rock face.

The technique of bark-painting, and also the fact that different types of art cannot be put into watertight compartments, are shown by an experience I had at Port Keats, on the Northern Australian coast, in 1954. At the mission there I asked the Murinbata natives if they would make bark paintings for me to illustrate the myths they had related. The natives told me that they had never made bark paintings. I asked them whether they would make me reproductions of their cave paintings, body paintings and designs on ceremonial objects if I showed them how to make a bark painting. They were only too ready and willing.

Naturally I did not have to show these tribesmen how to remove a sheet of bark from a tree, heat it by the fire, and lay it, smooth side down, on the ground with a stone on it so that it would dry out flat. But from then on I demonstrated what I had seen done by painters on the Roper River and at Milingimbi.

I asked my friends for some tree-orchid plants from the bush. I took one of the thick, fleshy stems of this plant, crushed one end and rubbed its liberal juice into the smooth inside surface of the sheet of bark to make the paint adhere. I then took red ochre and rubbed it into and over the juice that had been smeared on the smooth surface of the bark. The artist's 'canvas' was ready for painting. Then I made a brush by chewing and fraying one end of a stick, and stripped a sliver of bark for making fine lines, as I had seen my Roper River and Milingimbi teachers do. One demonstration was enough to set several artists in this tribe at work doing bark paintings.

An Aboriginal artist's paints are ochres, red and yellow. He also uses white clay and charcoal. These materials are ground and mixed with water. A hollow stone, a piece of curled bark, or a tin will hold his different paints.

The first paintings executed for me by the Murinbata tribe reminded me strongly of the motif and symbolic art of Central Australia. Some of the Murinbata myths were of ancestral beings who came from the sea and penetrated far inland to desert areas. I concluded there was a possible link between this coastal tribe and inland desert tribes.

Since my visit to Port Keats this centre has become one of the most prolific in producing bark paintings for sale in our southern cities and elsewhere. A few years ago I met a Murinbata friend of mine in Qantas House, Sydney, where he was on display executing bark paintings.

Murinbata art is now both representational and richly decorative with motifs and symbols. Outside influences have had their effect. The first paintings of this tribe that were brought to me were reproductions of their traditional sources.

The so-called X-ray paintings of north-eastern Arnhem Land are in the main representational. For example, a kangaroo is faithfully and fully reproduced but the backbone and internal organs are also painted. An artist will point out these organs, saying, 'This one, heart. This one, liver,' etc. Another feature of this art is its fine cross-hatching, executed in two or three colours. After the figures in the painting have been executed, the bodies and indeed the whole area of the painting may be filled in with this fine cross-hatching. In this type of painting, abstract designs and cross-hatching, can be motifs of clouds, falling rain, seaweed, sand, or waves. The art of motifs and symbols appears to be concentrated in Central Australian tribes. This traditional painting is representative of totemic emblems and their motifs. The designs are curvilinear: concentric circles, U-shaped figures, spirals, straight parallel lines and curved lines. These motifs could mean: concentric circles, camps of totemic ancestors;

Opposite
A Groote Eylandt
Aboriginal decorating a
bailer shell, NT.

A bark painting, showing the characteristic manganese black backgrounds of the Groote Eylandt artists.

Paintings and carvings from Groote Eylandt, NT, in which black manganese has been used.

Aboriginal totems or *ranggas* on Elcho Island, NT.

Traditional artefacts of the Elcho Island people, NT.

Cave paintings at Laura, about 140 kilometres
from Cooktown, Qld. These are some of the
best in Queensland, and show the male spirit of
fertility.

This cave contains important ship paintings of
Macassars. It was discovered on Groote Eylandt
by Nandjawarra and Douglass Baglin in 1967.

Rock paintings on Groote Eylandt, NT. The turtle painting is in red ochre outlined in white pipeclay, and there is also a stencilled hand in the picture. Hand stencils are made by filling the mouth with pigment mixed with water, placing the hand on the rock surface and spraying the 'paint' over and round it.

Birth of a child symbolised in cave paintings at
Elsharana, NT.

Rock engraving of shoal fish at West Head,
near Sydney, NSW. This was a totemic site of
fish and fertility rituals here ensured plentiful
supplies of fish for the Aboriginal inhabitants.

Rock engraving of anthropomorphic figure in
Ku-ring-gai Chase National Park, NSW. This
is doubtless the figure of an ancestral being
such as Barame the Sky-Father.

parallel straight lines, heaps of killed game; the U-shaped motif, a person sitting cross-legged on the ground.

This art, and indeed all Aboriginal art, is not to be viewed as we look at a painting, horizontally, at eye level. The picture is executed on the ground, and is to be seen vertically, from above and all round the painting. The use of symbols and motifs comes from tracks and imprints left on the ground by humans, animals, birds, reptiles, the remains of camp-sites, etc. Tracks and signs on the ground are more informative to an Aboriginal than a printed and illustrated book is to us.

Central Australian ground paintings, ritual head-dresses, body decorations, and decorated ritual objects, are strikingly beautiful forms of art.

Ground paintings have been observed among the northern and western Aranda Aboriginals of Central Australia, among the Unmatjera, the Pintubi, the Kukatja, the Pitjantjara, the Iliaura, and the Warramunga tribes of this region.

The surface for a ground painting was made from broken-up termite mound spread on the ground. This was softened with water and patted down. In many areas it was hardened by blood from the arm veins of men taking part in the ritual associated with the painting. The designs were executed in red and yellow ochre and charcoal, and in the white down of young eagles. Ten examples of these paintings are found in *Australian Aboriginal Decorative Art*, issued by the Australian Museum, Sydney.

Speaking of an Iliaura tribe ground painting of the honey-ant totem, T. G. H. Strehlow says, 'This ground painting was revealed to postulants as a verse from the relevant myth-cycle was sung. This compared the honey-filled storage ants, with their reddish bodies in the underground cells, to sleeping men, their bodies gleaming red in the glow of camp fires burning behind their windbreaks.'

Ritual head-dresses masked performers who, in the ritual, had assumed the personalities of the superhuman ancestral beings concerned. These impressive head-dresses were made of branch stems shaped, bent, and bound to the performers' heads, and covered and decorated with down in the appropriate motifs.

The sacred, ritual object Waningga, in the shape of a cross, or a double cross, and the totem pole Tnatantja, are other examples of Central Australian decorative art. In the myth of Ilia, the emu ancestor, Ilia was dancing a ritual, *tjurunga-andata*. 'He was dancing with the tall ceremonial pole, Tnatantja, thrust through his hair-belt at his back. He held the pole with his hands behind his back, and he was painted for the dancing, in red ochre and white feathers stuck on with blood from his feet right up to the crest of feathers on the top of the Tnatantja.'

In Central Australian areas where ground paintings were not made, painted shields were used for the same purpose of representing the totemic centres figuring in the ritual. The sacred *tjurunga*, which have previously been described, are slabs of stone or wood and are inscribed with the same type of motifs and symbols. A stone *tjurunga* of a desert yam totem site is inscribed with wavy parallel lines which indicate the long roots of desert yam bush. Parallel straight lines indicate new yam shoots. Crossed lines mean the leaves of the yam bush, and groups of dots depict the small yam bulbs.

Representational art, together with motifs, is generously represented in the Sydney-Hawkesbury sandstone area. In this region of sandstone ridges, gorges, open, low scrubby country, and rocky creekbeds, comprising some 900 square kilometres, over 600 groups or 'galleries' of rock engravings, containing over 4,000 figures, have been discovered.

Since the Aboriginals of this area were the first to come into contact with intensive settlement by the white man following the arrival of the First Fleet, little is known about these engravings. The tribes responsible for them are extinct and the best we can do is to interpret them through knowledge we have gained from living tribes.

Captain Watkin Tench, a member of the First Fleet, noted these engravings in the vicinity of Port Jackson. 'On many of the rocks,' he says, 'are also to be found delineations of the figures of men and birds, very poorly cut.'

Port Hedland, in northern Western Australia, is another area rich in rock-engravings. Here, over 15,000 figures are engraved on almost twelve kilometres of ridges. The main subjects are fish and boomerangs, but mammals, birds, reptiles and artifacts are included. Among the few ancestral beings or human figures is the anthropomorph, the so-called Minjiburu. Male and female human figures are represented, and the human figure is often in an alert or dancing posture. Pecked human tracks lead to the Minjiburu engravings. Turtle, dolphin, whale, ritual designs, weapons and sacred boards are included in the engravings.

Examples of rock-engravings are to be found from the north-western part of the continent, spreading south eastward into Central Australia, South Australia, and east into coastal New South Wales and Queensland.

One of the finest rock-galleries I have seen is in the bush on a height overlooking the sea some six or seven kilometres inland from Narrabeen, north of Sydney. These rock engravings are on flat, exposed areas of sandstone. The examples are mainly representational, the figures being pecked out in outline in a series of indentations, or in a continuous groove. The gallery contains the figure of a whale, two human figures with outstretched arms, a human figure carrying game on his back, three fishes swimming in line, and a number of circles.

The outline of the whale is huge, perhaps five metres in length, made round a natural swelling or mound in the rock surface. Standing on it, one sees the sea in the distance. One would say this was the totemic site of the whale, the swelling of the rock, its metamorphosed body. Whales are often grounded on this coast and on one occasion during the first years of the settlement at Port Jackson the Aboriginals feasted on a whale grounded on the beach inside the harbour at Manly.

F. D. McCarthy believes that some rock-engraved human figures in this area are ancestral beings. From what we know of Aboriginal art, animals, birds and fish represent totemic and fertility sites. Some of the sites are known to have been bora grounds, where initiation and sacred rituals were held.

One rock engraving at Maroota, upper Hawkesbury River, is a life-size figure of an emu with a clutch of eggs, and some engraved tracks. Below the emu is a round, natural waterhole in the rock surface. One would say that this waterhole was the totemic site of the emu. An Aboriginal woman on the Barwon River in New South Wales told me about an emu ancestor. A tribal elder had taken my informant and some of her friends down to the river to fish. 'He said to us, "Girls, don't make a noise now. You'll see that Ngoorimbalin coming down the bank directly."

'We were on a log, playing about. You know how mad silly girls play about, singing out.

'The tribal elder sang out, "*Ngark*, girls." That meant to tell us to look out. And we saw this big emu rolling the egg down the bank. He was going to put it in his nest, because the water-hole was his nest. That emu took the egg down with him. We call that hole in the river the Minga. That's the home of the emus.'

Bush-walking one day in a national park not far from Sydney, one of the brown or black scrub wallabies I often see in this area sprang out of the low scrub before me. I stopped to watch it bounding away through the scrub and found I was standing on a flat exposed rock surface on which was engraved a scrub wallaby.

Some years ago I was asked to see some rock engravings near Narrabeen where land development was taking place. A road was being made through an area of rock engravings. A circle slab of rock with a bounding kangaroo, beautifully executed, had been cut out of the rock with jack-hammers. The circle slab was broken in two, no doubt as the result of efforts made to lift it on to a truck and take it away.

Not far from the road we found a rock face where engraved fishes' tails showed out from under tea-tree bushes growing over the rock. Lifting back the bushes, we found the complete fishes, which were about a metre in length. Enlightened and interested people have had most of the rock engravings in the standstone area declared protected sites, although one such protected site I have seen has its protective rail-fence posts sunk into the rock across an engraving.

The carved trees of New South Wales are another form of Aboriginal art concerning which little is known. These were trees on which an area of bark was cut away, usually in a long oval shape. The exposed area was then carved in an integrated series of geometric designs or motifs. Settlement and land clearing have destroyed most of these trees, although the Australian Museum has in its possession a varied range of these tree-trunk sections containing the carvings. Little more can be said of these trees than that they were of ceremonial importance to the Aboriginals who carved them.

Carved wooden figures, used in sacred rituals, were made in north-eastern Arnhem Land. Examples of such wood carvings are the two Wawalag Sisters, ancestral beings of the Wawalag myth. These figures are painted in motifs relating to their creative behaviour and significance.

Another is the figure of the ancestral being Laindjun, also similarly painted. This figure is decorated with seagull and parakeet feathers. The sacred patterns on the body are freshwater weed design, fire and ashes inside seaweed and mud, hollow log under water, stripped bark, red ochre and cliffs, spring water, wild bees and honeycomb, mangrove worm and hollow log, wild bees, ashes and honeycomb. These figures are on permanent loan to the Australian Institute of Anatomy, Canberra.

The carved and painted grave-posts of the Aboriginals of Bathurst and Melville Islands of the Northern Territory are another striking example of Aboriginal carving. I first saw these grave-posts in the bush near the Katherine River where they were pointed out to me by the late W. E. Harney, the writer and authority on the Aboriginals. 'Bilarni', as he was known, explained that they were erected by Melville Island Aboriginals for relatives who had died while working in that area during the last war.

In 1958 a collection of such grave-posts was acquired by the New South Wales Art Gallery. The seventeen sculptural grave-posts are part of the Pukamuni mourning ritual. In many cases the Melville and Bathurst Island grave-posts are carved human figures in a highly stylised form, in some cases the deceased person himself, in others, his immediate relatives. They are richly and dramatically painted in geometric designs and motifs of ritual and mythical significance.

I have seen many beautiful examples of carved wooden figures made by the Aboriginals of Goulburn Island, Arnhem Land. Their carvings of fish, birds, animals, etc, reminded me of the imaginative, compact and stylised sculpture of the Eskimos. The Goulburn Island Aboriginals have taken advantage of the wood-turning lathes installed at their Mission to fashion these figures.

Such carvings, together with an outpouring of bark paintings and various examples of Aboriginal handcrafts, provide a source of income to the missions and settlements from the outside world. The bark paintings executed for such commercial purpose are non-sacred paintings, or paintings from which anything offensive to civilised white people has been excised. Already they show the results of mass production and commercialism. They are not produced with religious reverence and artistry, as are the sacred or religious paintings.

The story of Albert Namatjira, the Aranda tribesman who became world-famous for his water-colours of Central Australian landscapes carried out in a European tradition, is well-known.

Namatjira was camel boy and camp cook to the painter Rex Battarbee on painting locations in Central Australia. The Aboriginal observed the white man at work and tried out the technique of water-colours. Rex Battarbee encouraged his camel boy with the result that Albert Namatjira paintings became popular.

The water-colours of Albert Namatjira faithfully record the colourful and dramatic desert landscapes, their ranges, dry watercourses and stony expanses of spinifex and stunted scrub, their startling ghost-gums which became a repetitive signature to a Namatjira painting, their desert oaks and 'dead finish' trees.

Naturally, Namatjira, as a tribesman, knew his landscapes intimately, but there is no hint of mythical and religious meaning in his paintings. That he was a draughtsman and colourist of great skill there is no doubt, but he is not regarded as having made any contribution to European art. A popular painter, he is sparsely represented in Australian national galleries.

I once discussed with Albert Namatjira the possibility of his reproducing his tribal painting of motifs and symbols. Since bark paintings of tribal art have been acquired by the national galleries, Central Australian tribal art should have found its rightful recognition. Albert Namatjira did not live long enough to carry out such a suggestion.

Other Aranda painters, sometimes known as the 'Hermansburg School' from the Lutheran mission of Hermansburg in Central Australia, have carried on the practice of Albert Namatjira. The work of such painters as Edwin and Otto Pareroultja shows a much more primitive or tribal feeling for landscape than the faithfully representational art of Namatjira.

From what I have seen, Aboriginals possess a natural ability for draughtsmanship and colour. I first met Namatjira's son Evald at Areyonga. He was sketching in the rock faces and peaks of part of the gorge with masterly draughtsmanship. At the time I did not know who he was. Later, he told me that his father was coming to Areyonga and would paint in the sketches he had made. Purists among white people might object to this practice. Actually, a ground painting may be executed by several 'artists'. In this case they are merely executing traditional patterns that have existed unchanged for hundreds, perhaps thousands, of years.

A striking bark painting of a cormorant was once made for me on the Roper River. The Aboriginal artist who brought the painting to me told me that I would have to pay him twice for the painting. When I asked him why this was he told me that the painting had been done by him and another Aboriginal. The cormorant had a red body dotted over in white and I asked the artist which part of the painting he had done. He said that he had painted the body, and that his companion had put in the white dots.

One may find humour in this situation, but it is often a traditional method for two men to work together to carry out a traditional painting.

8 The impact of the white man

The first Europeans who are known to have seen
Australia were Dutchmen. In 1606, the *Duyfken*
(little dove) commanded by Janszoon, sailed part of
the way down the western coast of Cape York
Peninsula. The Dutchmen were not pleased with
what they saw: 'Nowhere was there any sign of gold,
or any promise of trade.' Later Dutchmen, following
the *Duyfken's* course, said, 'We found nothing but
wild coasts, barren land, and extremely cruel, savage,
and barbarous natives.'

When Captain Cook sighted the unknown southern coast of the continent in
1770 and sailed north along it he found a 'Bay which appeared to be tolerably well
sheltered from all winds.' He sailed in. Later he called it Botany Bay.

From the anchorage of their ship, the *Endeavour*, the white men watched
natives cook their fish on the beach. Then a party of Englishmen rowed towards
the land. As they drew near, two Aboriginals stood near the water's edge to
oppose them. The Englishmen tried to parley with them, but to no avail. The
Aboriginals threw their spears at the landing boat, and the Englishmen fired
muskets loaded with small shot. The two Aboriginals ran away at the sound of
the muskets. With no more opposition than this, Cook and his party landed on
the beach of the Land of Baiame.

From the scrub behind the sandhills the Aboriginals watched the white men.
Cook and his men found some children crouched in a *mia-mia*. They threw beads
to the frightened children and walked on, unmolested.

After eight days in what the botanist Joseph Banks described as a 'botanist's
paradise', Cook sailed away. Eighteen years later, the First Fleet, eleven ships
under the command of Captain Arthur Phillip, arrived at Botany Bay.

A few days later, at Sydney Cove, in 'one of the best harbours in the world', the
colony of New South Wales was established. The Union Jack was flown from a
flagstaff, volleys of musketry were fired, and men drank to the health of the King
and the prosperity of the new colony. The possession of the Land of Baiame by
the white men had begun.

Captain Phillip, the governor of the colony, bearing tremendous respon-
sibilities, was a humane and just man. It was his wish to make friends with the
Aboriginals and, if possible, to understand them. Captain Watkin Tench, an
officer in the colony, noted in his journal Sydney's First Four Years, the
difficulties attending this aim.

1788. With the natives we were very little more acquainted than on our
arrival in the country. Our intercourse with them was neither frequent nor
cordial. They seemed studiously to avoid us, either from fear, jealousy, or
hatred. When they met with unarmed stragglers they sometimes killed, and

sometimes wounded them. I confess that, in common with many others, I was inclined to attribute this conduct to a spirit of malignant levity. But a further acquaintance with them, founded on several instances of their humanity and generosity, which shall be noted in their proper places, has entirely reversed my opinion; and led me to conclude, that the unproved outrages committed upon them, by unprincipled individuals among us, caused the evils we had experienced.

The country around Port Jackson, the early name for Sydney Harbour, appears to have been the country of Aboriginal clans under such tribal names as the Gweagal, the Wanngal, the Cammeraygal etc. The story of the Aboriginal Bennelong, of the Wanngal group which inhabited the southern shore of the harbour where the settlement was established, is the story of the first attempt by white men to assimilate or integrate the Aboriginals.

Following the disappearance of a soldier and several convicts, three convicts wounded, and one killed near Botany Bay, Governor Phillip decided to capture some of the Aboriginals. The purpose of this intention was, as Tench explains, to 'induce an intercourse, by the report which our prisoners would make of the mildness and indulgence with which we used them. And farther, it promised to unveil the cause of their mysterious conduct, by putting us in possession of their reasons for harassing and destroying our people.'

At Manly Cove a party of marines enticed a group of Aboriginals with presents and a show of friendship. The marines then rushed the natives and succeeded in capturing one, a man named Arabanoo. Although a captive, Arabanoo was well treated by the white men. It is recorded that

> his character was distinguished by a portion of gravity and steadiness . . . His countenance was thoughtful, but not animated: his fidelity and gratitude, particularly to his friend the governor, were constant and undeviating. Although of a placable and gentle temper, we early discovered that he was impatient of indignity, and allowed no superiority on our part. If the slightest insult were offered him, he would return it with interest.
>
> At retaliation of merriment he was often happy; and frequently turned the laugh against his antagonist. He did not want docility; but either from the difficulty of acquiring our language, from the unskilfulness of his teachers, or from some natural defect, his progress in learning was not equal to what we had expected. For the last three or four weeks of his life hardly any restraint was laid upon his inclinations, so that had he meditated escape he might easily have effected it. He was, perhaps, the only native who was ever attached to us by choice; and who did not prefer a precarious existence among wilds and precipices, to the comforts of a civilised system.

After five months with the white men, Arabanoo died from the smallpox which, brought to the country by the white man, swept through the Aboriginals, who had no resistance to this new disease, and slaughtered them.

Phillip and his men did all they could for the Aboriginals dying in the bush around them and along the foreshores of the harbour. Two children were acquired and adopted by the settlement, a girl, Abaroo, and a boy, Nanbaree. Both these children had lost their parents through the smallpox.

Later, two more Aboriginals were captured, Bennelong and Col-bee. Col-bee escaped, but Bennelong remained to become the favourite of the Governor. Bennelong was intelligent and talented. He soon learned to speak English and to adopt the white man's manners and dress. He sat at the Governor's table, and came and went to and from the Governor's house as he pleased.

When Phillip returned to England, he took Bennelong and another Aboriginal named Imeerawanyee with him. The two Aboriginals were presented to the King. Imeerawanyee died in England, but Bennelong returned to the colony with Governor Hunter.

Bennelong appears to have been a high-spirited, good-natured and colourful individual. He was vain and proud of his position among the white man. He returned to the colony in powdered wig, jacket, cravat, breeches, stockings and shoes. From the porch of Government House he lectured his naked people on the need to adopt the white man's manners and dress. The tribesmen mocked him.

It was not long before Bennelong had thrown off his finery and returned to the tribal way of life. He was an example of the Aboriginal torn between the surface attractions of the white man's civilisation and the real security of his tribal life. He had acquired an addiction to wine and spirits, and became a nuisance to the white men. Eventually he found the Governor's door shut against him, with a soldier barring the way.

Bennelong became an outcast, wandering in a limbo between two worlds. He was shockingly wounded and mutilated in a tribal fight and Governor Hunter placed him on board a ship in the harbour to protect him. Bennelong returned to his tribal country and it is not known what became of him.

Although the township at Port Jackson was a convict settlement, Britain's answer to her harsh laws which produced 1,000 convicts a year, Phillip had something bigger in mind when he brought the First Fleet out to Australia. He visualised a new British nation overseas. Within his four years as governor, exploration and expansion had established the farming settlement of Rose Hill at Parramatta.

By 1793 the white men were trying to find a way over the inland barrier of the Blue Mountains. In 1813 Gregory Blaxland, a wealthy grazier, William Lawson, and William Charles Wentworth, also interested in grazing, found the ridge which led them over this barrier of gorges and sheer cliffs to the foothills leading to the western plains beyond. The penetration of the continent had begun.

An Aboriginal of a rather different character to Bennelong figured in the history of the initial phase of white settlement in Western Australia. This Aboriginal was Yagan of the Bibbulmun tribe on the Swan River. Yagan's tribe at first welcomed the white men, believing them to be the spirits of their dead returned to them.

Between the governor of the colony, Captain Stirling, and Yagan, a natural leader of his people, a friendship of mutual trust and respect was established. Realising the material superiority of the whites, Yagan tried to reconcile the two opposing civilisations but soon found himself in the difficult position of having to try to make the whites recognise the justice of his tribal law that 'paid back' the shooting of a tribesman with the spearing of a white man.

Yagan did not act without justification. Indeed, he was called 'the courteous savage'. The editor of the *Perth Gazette* likened him to the famous Scottish patriot Wallace, defending his country and the rights of his people. The editor concluded his article, 'What will he do next, this strange, vindictive, but always courteous savage?'

Yagan became an outlaw with a price of £30 on his head. Two white boys shot him while pretending to go hunting kangaroos with him. Their motive was the price on the head of their Aboriginal friend.

There was no organised resistance by the Aboriginals to the white man's invasion, exploration and settlement of their country as compared with the

Maori resistance in New Zealand. Scattered over the continent, few in numbers, nomadic hunters and food-gatherers, the Aboriginals had not reached the stage of being agriculturalists or keepers of flocks and herds which makes sustained and organised warfare possible. The Aboriginals had inter-clan and inter-tribal warfare, but these differences were not caused by needs or desires for material or territorial gains. The differences were caused by violation of tribal laws, or by personal feuds. As the preceding chapters have shown, the Aboriginals were bound to their 'countries' by the religious and spiritual ties of their Dreamtime, or Creation time.

The kind of resistance of which the Aboriginals were capable, and also the friendship they extended to the white man, are recorded in the accounts of the explorers. During Charles Sturt and his party's journey in a boat down the Murray River, the following incident took place.

> At one place the party was near disaster. The river narrowed down, and on the bank there was gathered a mob of hundreds of natives armed for war, their spears quivering in their grasp ready to hurl. Sturt prepared for the worst. He decided to shoot the leader in the hope that his fall would scare the rest, so that the boat could pass in peace.
>
> Just as his finger lay on the trigger, four natives appeared on the opposite bank. One was a man with whom Sturt had previously made friends. This native plunged into the river and swam across to the warlike band. He took the leader by the throat and pushed him back from the attack; he stamped on the sand, and harangued the crowd. He succeeded in calming them, and before long Englishmen and natives were friends, and Sturt could give a suitable present to the man who had saved him from disaster.

Other instances of Aboriginal friendship to the white man are those of Wylie, the faithful companion of the explorer Edward John Eyre, and Jacky-Jacky, the only member of the explorer E. B. Kennedy's tragic party to survive and reach the destination of Cape York at the tip of the Peninsula.

The only surviving member of the Burke and Wills expedition of 1860, the white man J. King, was befriended and cared for by an Aboriginal tribe until he was found by a search party.

That the Aboriginals considered they could live with the white man is borne out by the 'sale' of about 240,000 hectares of land at Port Phillip in 1835 by the Aboriginals to the settler John Batman. The price of this land was 40 pairs of blankets, 42 tomahawks, 130 knives, 62 pairs of scissors, 40 looking-glasses, 250 handkerchiefs, 150 lbs of flour, 22 shirts and 4 suits of clothes. He also promised to pay them a yearly tribute of 150 pairs of blankets, 150 knives, 150 tomahawks, 70 suits of clothes, 50 looking-glasses, 100 pairs of scissors and 70 tons of flour.

Batman, who had always been a good friend to the Aboriginals, was almost alone among the pioneers in making some payment to the natives in return for the hunting grounds he was taking from them. The document was signed by John Batman, and eight natives made their mark upon it.

This was a sincere act on the part of the white man, but the Aboriginals could not and did not know what the 'sale' meant. Naturally they understood that they would remain on their hunting and totemic grounds and merely let the white man's flocks and herds have the grass, which was in abundance. They could neither understand nor foresee the state of affairs expressed in a 'transitional' Aboriginal song: 'Huntin' food was Jacky's business, till the white man came along, ran the fences across his country. Now the huntin' days are gone.'

Generally speaking, the white man's annexation of the Aboriginals' tribal

Opposite
Aboriginals taking part in the re-enactment of the Captain Cook landing at Kurnell, Sydney, in 1970.

Examples of Bathurst Island art: a carved and painted ceremonial spearhead, two carved and painted human figures, two carved and painted snakes, a crocodile and a club.

Aboriginal stockmen with children, playing with a captive turtle at Mornington Island, Gulf of Carpentaria.

Opposite   Shearing sheep in Dubbo, NSW.

Aboriginal life outside government or mission influence at Caledon Bay, NT, their buildings of bark blend into the surroundings.

An artists' camp at Yirrkala, NT. This is where
paintings on bark are done.

Two birds and busts of human figures, carved
from wood and painted with totemic designs,
from Groote Eylandt, Gulf of Carpentaria.

The first Europeans who were known to have seen Australia were Dutchmen. In March 1606 the *Duyfken* sailed part of the way down the western coast of Cape York Peninsula. This painted stone at Duyfken Point, Gulf of Carpentaria, commemorates the landing of the Dutch and the Aboriginals' first contact with Europeans.

Man with a bark painting of abstract design. It illustrates the myth of the north-east wind. This is from Groote Eylandt.

Red ochre painting of a horse near Cooktown,
Qld. Local belief is that the painting represents
a horse first seen in the region by the
Aboriginals during the journey of the explorer
Kennedy.

A crocodile, carved from wood and painted,
from Bathurst Island.

countries meant the annihilation of the natives. The *Australian Encyclopedia* writes that '. . . many natives were poisoned by arsenic mixed in flour, or inserted in the carcass of a sheep.' In evidence before a NSW Legislative Council Committee on the Aborigines Question in 1838, the Rev L. E. Threlkeld told of Aboriginals being decoyed into a hut and butchered as they came out one at a time, and of another group (men, women and children) being massacred by stockmen as they were peacefully gathering bark. Before the same Committee, Lieut R. Sadleir, RN, said that 'the natives have to endure a variety of wrongs, without any means of redress, but by retaliation'. He referred to 'most atrocious acts of violence on both sides, but more especially inexcusable on the part of the whites, who have in several instances practised barbarities on these people, revolting to human nature, which have been overlooked . . .'

THE IMPACT OF THE WHITE MAN

The history of the occupation of Tasmania by the whites and the subsequent complete annihilation of the Aboriginal population is one which few white people care to linger over. I have had a place pointed out to me in Tasmania, on the north coast, where hundreds of Aboriginals were driven to a cliff—where women with their children in their arms, and men, leapt over the cliff to their deaths on the rocks below, rather than face the rifles of the white men in their 'Black Drive'. I have a list of interviews with tribal Aboriginals and dispossessed Aboriginals who have related the stories of massacres on the mainland to me. In two instances the narrators were the only survivors of their tribes. They were taken as babies by white men and reared by them to become shepherds and stockmen.

Following the reports of the explorers of their discoveries of good land, rivers, and lagoons, the settlers arrived with their bullock-drawn wagons, their families, their horses, and flocks or herds. The settlers occupied vast areas of the tribal lands. The Aboriginals were no more to them than part of the objectionable fauna and flora which had to be removed to make the land suitable for their flocks and herds.

When the Aboriginals, 'who were too primitive to be civilised', retaliated, the settlers joined forces in punitive expeditions against them. In most cases these expeditions set out not merely to pacify the troublesome and vengeful natives, but to be rid of the problem by exterminating them. From 1840 to 1880 the settlers, who were represented in the Governments' Legislative Councils, and later in the Legislative Assemblies, received indirect recognition for this 'pacification by force' of the Aboriginals.

One of the most effective means employed in this 'pacification' was the use of bodies of Aboriginal police troopers. The first troop of native police was formed when an English ex-army officer, Henry Dana, enrolled twenty-five recruits at Port Phillip in 1842. The native police wore green jackets with possum-skin facings, black trousers with red stripes, and green caps with red bands. They were drilled and trained to become 'reasonable marksmen'. They were mounted police, and were excellent horsemen and trackers.

The famous, or infamous, Queensland black police were formed in 1849. This was a case of using the Aboriginals, with their superior knowledge of the country and of Aboriginal behaviour, to exterminate their own people. The black police were savagely effective. They could use their authority and, armed with the white man's rifles, took the opportunity to settle for ever old tribal scores and feuds.

An Aboriginal of the New England district, New South Wales, told me that, 'in those days, 1880, every station had a team of Aboriginals in military clothes. They were bare-footed, and they wore trousers with a red stripe down them. They were armed with muzzle-loaders and Martini-Henrys'. In the account my informant

93

gave me, an Aboriginal militia accompanied a Mr Jordon, the manager of Tabulam Station, to capture an Aboriginal suspected of murder, who was at Kyogle station. The Aboriginal militia regarded the expedition as a tribal *girravul*, 'an Aboriginal raiding party which would take back with it all the women of the tribe they would attack and clean out. And this was why Jordon's Aborigines had been so eager to come with him.'

An old Aboriginal of the Clarence River also told me about the black police. He said, 'There were thousands of wild people [Aboriginals]. My mother was half wild. All the white people and the black police shot them. People won't believe it today. I've argued with the police sergeant here at Bowraville about it.'

By 1845 the tribes between Broken Bay and Botany Bay, once numbering 1,500 or more, were practically extinct, and a man and three women were all that were left of the tribe occupying the southern shores of Port Jackson, which had numbered 400 in the days of Governor Macquarie (1810-21). For the whole of Australia, the estimated number of Aboriginals in 1961 was about 50,000.

Punitive expeditions, and such brutal actions as stockwhip floggings in dealing with the Aboriginals in the sparsely settled central, north-western and northern areas of the continent, actually persisted until the 1930s.

As early as 1836, reports of the treatment of the Aboriginals and their plight had reached England and resulted in the formation of movements such as the Aborigines Protection Society in England and the Select Committee on Aboriginal Tribes in British Settlements.

The new governor of South Australia, Governor Gawler, immediately on landing, issued a proclamation declaring that 'the Aboriginal inhabitants of this province, throughout its wide extent, were to be considered as British subjects'.

In 1839 Matthew Moorhouse became the first official Protector of the Aborigines. Ignorant and misguided though it was, it was an official and humane attempt at the long process of assimilation or integration of the Aboriginals. An indication of the lack of understanding of the gulf which existed between the white man's civilisation and the Aboriginals' way of life is summed up in the speech with Moorhouse gave at a goodwill party given to the natives on the Queen's Birthday in 1838:

> Black men—
> We wish to make you happy. But you cannot be happy unless you imitate good white men. Build huts, wear clothes, work and be useful. Above all you cannot be happy unless you love God who made heaven and earth and men and all things.
> Love white men. Love other tribes of black men. Do not quarrel together. Tell other tribes to love white men, and to build good huts and wear clothes. Learn to speak English.
> If any white man injures you, tell the Protector and he will do you justice.

In State after State, protection policies were implemented in attempts to provide the 'fringe-dwellers' around country towns with rations, blankets and medicine. Victoria began with its policy in 1860, Western Australia in 1886, Queensland in 1897, New South Wales in 1909, and the Northern Territory in 1911.

In the period between these early protection policies and the present day there have been four stages of official attitude towards the Aboriginals. The aim of the first period was the assimilation of the Aboriginals. The native people were to be given all the benefits of British justice and equality.

When the problems of assimilation made themselves evident, attitudes of resignation and despair took the place of the early enthusiastic ideal of assimilation. The Aboriginals were rapidly dying out and officials believed that soon there would be no Aboriginal problem to be concerned about.

Towards the end of the nineteenth century reserves and missions for the Aboriginals were established. This action, in spite of the prevailing belief that it was to 'smooth the pillow of a dying race', gave the natives protection and at least a breathing space, even though this breath was one of resignation and despair.

By 1911 a policy of strict segregation was put into practice. Again, although this kind of protection—segregation, and charity—made the dispossessed Aboriginals into 'intelligent parasites', it did halt the process of the dying out of the race and, by its negative attitude, prepared the way for the emergence of the modern Aboriginal.

After the Conference of Commonwealth and State Aboriginal authorities in 1937, there was a considerably enlightened attitude towards the policy of assimilation.

Today it can be said that the Aboriginals are showing definite signs of saving themselves. Throughout the continent they are forming their own organisations, finding their own leaders, in place of sympathetic white people of the past, and taking matters into their own hands. It can be said that both the tribal Aboriginals mainly in the Arnhem Land Reserve, and the dispossessed Aboriginals do not seek assimilation but integration.

Many Aboriginals today are no longer ashamed of being Aboriginals. Their racial pride has awakened. They wish to live, as other racial groups do—the Jewish, the Italian, the Greek—with their own identity and culture, as fellow citizens in the Australian community.

Behind this summary of events lies a long and protracted struggle. The impact of the white man was a devastating blow. It deprived the Aboriginals of their 'countries', their culture and identity, the security of their tribal life. In their struggle to survive, many nameless as well as known Aboriginal leaders have played their part, as have indignant and sympathetic white people. Many missionaries, and here the German Lutherans must be specially named, have struggled in the cause of the Aboriginals. Without the work of anthropologists from 1870 to the present day we could never have understood the Aboriginals and found a common means of communication.

Writers and people such as Daisy Bates, who gave her life to helping the Aboriginals and wrote of her experiences, Mrs K. Langloh Parker, and R. H. Mathews who recorded early oral traditions, novelists such as Eleanor Dark, Katharine Susannah Pritchard, and Nene Gare, have all roused the conscience of white people and contributed to the emergence of the modern Aboriginal.

THE IMPACT OF THE
WHITE MAN

9 The Aboriginals today

It was trading day for the Aboriginals at Milingimbi Mission in the Crocodile Islands. Huge shady tamarind trees, planted long ago by the *bêche-de-mer*-gathering Macassars, lined the yellow crescent of the beach. The full incoming tide of the pale-green Arafura Sea lay calm, brimming, lazily lapping and hissing, along the sand.

But the bare, trodden, sun- and shadow-mottled space around the store and under the trees was crowded with expectant Aboriginals. The women, always naked to the waist, wore mission-material skirts of apricot, mauve, red and yellow. The younger men wore loin-cloths of varying colours but the old men, with their traditional tufts of beards, often wore an old pair of shorts, or a *naga*, a strip of cloth hanging in front from the waist.

The children, especially the very young, ran about quite naked. I remember one little boy with a vivid yellow ochre fish painted diagonally across the chocolate brown of his stomach. The fish seemed alive, undulating and breathing with the little boy's movements.

The Aboriginals stood about in groups, talking among themselves. Families and the more primitive groups, the bush-Aboriginals, kept themselves apart, sitting or standing, watching, among the trees. They were waiting for the store to open, and they had with them examples of their arts and crafts on which they had been working from time to time for the past week.

At the store, a big galvanised-iron shed, the missionary's wife would value the articles, the Aboriginals would then buy tea, sugar, flour, tinned foods, lengths of dress material, knives, axes and tobacco. The women had large circular mats, dillybags, and all kinds of shopping baskets woven from pandanus fibre. The men had brought paintings and carvings, miniature canoes, and painted spears and boomerangs.

Every six weeks or so a lugger would come round the perilous coast from Darwin and unload its cargo at the beach. Two hundred-litre drums of petrol were just tipped into the water and allowed to wash up on to the beach. After a couple of days the lugger loaded with the Mission's arts and crafts would depart for Darwin, where they would be sold to tourists.

Some time previously I had seen the mission lugger arrive and anchor off the beach. It had come from Goulburn Island and was both engine-powered and driven by sail. I was amazed to find that its crew was comprised entirely of Aboriginals from Goulburn Island, and these included the captain and the engineer. Manned by its native crew, the lugger had been plying for years along the coast without a single mishap. On this occasion the lugger brought the mission's head carpenter, a full-blood Aboriginal who was going to repair boats and do building work at Milingimbi.

I was sitting on a log on the outskirts of the crowd with old Johnny Dai-ngung-ngung. Johnny called me his son; he was my narrator and translator of the myths I was gathering. Now Johnny rose and signed to me to follow him. Reaching the farther side of the crowd, he said, 'Bush-blackfeller come up. 'Im friend belong me.'

There was a cool wind blowing. I did not see them at first but crouching and sitting in the deep shade was a group of naked Aboriginals. We came up to them and Johnny sat down among them. I sat on one heel near Johnny. These Aboriginals were young men, crocodile hunters. They had broad, clean, lightly-bearded faces with pronounced cheekbones, and their hair came down to their shoulders in long, greased, twisted strands. One man, crouching with one knee under his chin, shivered like an animal in the cool wind as he crouched, listening. These men wore only hair-belts of plaited human hair, with a pearl-shell pendant in front. Their weapons, spear-throwers and shovel-nosed spears, lay on the ground beside their hands.

Only now and then could I catch a word that I understood, but I knew that Johnny was one of the old men at Milingimbi with authority and sacred knowledge. He was not talking to these men merely of the bargain the missionary would drive for their crocodile skins. He told me that these old men did not smoke our tobacco nor did they want our tucker. ' 'Im savvy bush-tucker,' said Johnny. They wanted a tomahawk, and iron for spears. They belonged to the jungle and the tortuous mangrove-lined rivers.

Johnny told me that these men would not remain at the mission. When they had sold their crocodile skins and got what they wanted in return, they would go. 'This place only rubbish-place to 'im' Johnny explained. ' 'Im go back along 'im country.'

I had gone into the store to look over the paintings that were coming in. Two Aboriginal women were assisting Mrs Bell, the missionary's wife, with the trading. Outside, under the raised flap of the counter window, there was a babel of excitedly talking and trading natives. Then one woman's voice was raised above the rest. As though this outburst was expected, the others fell silent.

The speaker was Ginjineir. Years ago she had voyaged with her husband in a canoe round the hundreds of miles of perilous coast to Darwin. The husband had died in Darwin with 'the cough', and his widow had stayed and worked in a white woman's house and had often been to the shop of Aboriginal arts and crafts. There, being an interested and intelligent woman, she had noted the prices that her people's paintings, mats and baskets were bringing.

These prices, naturally far in excess of the payments made to her people for creating the articles, had roused Ginjineir to anger. Now, having lately returned to the mission, she had chosen her time to give Mrs Bell the benefit of her knowledge. Mrs Bell, confronted with the facts of the glaring differences between Darwin and Milingimbi prices, tried to explain and defend herself.

I had seen these 'battles of wits' between intelligent Aboriginals and white people before. Mrs Bell, attacked before all the people, was clearly at a disadvantage. As the discussion progressed, and the native woman methodically destroyed every one of the white woman's defences, Mrs Bell made the mistake of resorting to tears.

'All-about bin angry, missus. You bin cheat 'em along these baskets,' said Ginjineir.

'Don't you dare talk to me like that, Ginjineir. You don't understand,' retorted Mrs Bell, beginning to get angry also.

'Me savvy all right. You want to pay all-about more. All-about savvy you bin sell 'em along Birwin for twenty-five tchillin', an' you bin pay all-about one tchillin'.'

'You don't understand,' explained Mrs Bell. 'All that money comes back here to build up this mission for you and your people.'

'Which way that money come back along mission?' the Aboriginal woman argued. 'No more. You bin cheat all-about along these baskets.'

'Oh, how can you talk like that?' Mrs Bell answered, beginning to search for her handkerchief. 'You know Mr Bell and I came here to build up this mission for you people and for—' At this point she burst into tears.

But Ginjineir was not to be placated by tears. Shaking her finger in the white woman's face, she said, 'No more you little-bit cry, missus, Ar not bin tell you properly yet.'

Rallying herself, Mrs Bell dried her tears. 'Look, Ginjineir, Mr Bell has explained all this before to you. You don't want to understand. Now, will you please let us get on with the trading?'

Many of the women had their mats and baskets on the counter, waiting for the argument to finish. It seemed that 'all-about' thought Ginjineir had had her say. Ginjineir left the counter, calling over her shoulder as she did so, 'All-a-time we bin row about this. Ar no more bin tell you properly yet.'

A painted drone-pipe which one Aboriginal handed in took my eye. Its motif of caterpillars and leaves, repeated lengthways all round the pipe in traditional manner, made a rich effect in its fresh ochre colours. I went round to this man and told him how much I liked his painting. I asked him if he could do the same painting on flat bark as the drone-pipe was too heavy to take back to my country. 'Yoo,' he answered, 'make 'im properly.'

By midday the main business at the store was finished. During the afternoon occasional purchases were made by the Aboriginals with the silver paid to them for their arts and crafts. I came back to see how my painting was shaping and found the artist waiting for me with the finished painting. I liked it very much and paid the Aboriginal in silver. As I walked down through the camp to find Johnny, I saw the dancers.

In the sandy earth, three girls were dancing in line. They danced facing a splendidly-built young Aboriginal who gave them the song, the beat and rhythm, as he sang and hit the two songsticks together. The songman was Leodardi, one of the many sons of the tribally powerful old man, Weltjenmirree.

That evening, it seemed, the camp was happy and contented. The old people had tobacco which they smoked either in a crab's claw or in the long, straight smoking pipe with its cartridge-shell bowl. The women, especially the young ones, had new lengths of bright dress material. The children were happy with boiled lollies, and sometimes a tin of fruit or jam. In the camp, fires were flickering and tea was being boiled or, rather, stewed. A cool wind kept the mosquitoes away. It was a good night for singing and dancing.

That evening we saw and heard many dances and songs performed by the young people in the camp. These were camp dances and songs, many of which came from far-off places like Elcho Island and Goulburn Island. They were popular song-dances, and we sat in the dust with the older people and kept time to the dancing and singing with our clapping hands.

The tide was ebbing as we walked back along the beach to our own camp. A long, incoming wave, its curving hollow filled with a shoal of reflected stars, rose, curled, and with long low thunder spent itself. A Macassar-type canoe, which had brought other island visitors to Milingimbi for the trading day, lay on its side on the beach. Occasionally luminescent tongues of the waves ran up, hissing and licking along its sides.

The foregoing scene is fairly typical of Aboriginals living in their tribal country, contained in a reserve and in contact with civilisation through an established mission. The Methodist Mission at Milingimbi, like other missions established on similar reserves, prepares and equips, through education and experience of the better aspects of our civilisation, the rising generations of the Aboriginals with knowledge that will enable them to meet the inevitable inroads and changes which white society must bring.

Few people realise that the Aboriginal reserves are not inviolate. In a statement provided by Senator Spooner in reply to a question in Parliament in 1963, this passage occurs: 'Aborigines do not have land tenure rights over areas set aside as reserves. Under Northern Territory law all mineral and forestry rights are reserved to the Crown and royalties are determined by Legislature'. *(Hansard)*

Mining interests have for some time invaded the Arnhem Land Reserve. In August 1963, a unique petition on bark was addressed to the House of Representatives. Its text, written in English and in dialect, requested the Parliament to appoint a committee with interpreters to hear the views of the Yirrkala Aboriginals in Arnhem Land before firm arrangements were entered into with any mining company. When this bark petition was questioned, an identical petition arrived a week later over the signatures of Aboriginals whose authority was beyond question.

On 12 September it was announced that the Government would accede to the request of the Yirrkala petitioners. In this particular case the mining interest, a foreign one, withdrew its application for mining leases. But a precedent had been established: in future, tribal Aboriginals would be consulted in these matters. Furthermore, monetary compensations would be paid to the Aboriginal people in the event of mining companies operating in the Reserve. This is a far cry from the time when the white man simply dispossessed the Aboriginals of their country and brutally eliminated them in the process.

Another inspiring if less happy picture is of Aboriginals in north-western Australia. Under the leadership of a white man, Don McLeod, they set up their own mining and pastoral co-operatives. Their story is a long one but, briefly, they were dispossessed natives who had walked off stations where they worked as stockmen etc, in a strike for better conditions.

I visited this co-operative some years ago when I came into the area from the Kimberleys. The country was in an unbelievable profusion of wild flowers.

I am looking for the Aboriginal mining co-operative, Nomads Pty Ltd, and the white man Don McLeod. Through the spinifex, against a background of rocky hills, three Aboriginals are walking. An old woman is walking alone in the rear. The leading Aboriginal points me on down the track. I come on to the camp, a scattered cluster of shacks, tents and windbreaks among low, surrounding hills. At the back of the camp a tall water-boring plant stands.

McLeod's hut is a low galvanised-iron hut with no windows and a doorless entrance. It is built of bushtimber. In a far corner a man is lying down on canvas on the red earth floor. Boxes filled with papers, books and mineral specimens are stacked around the canvas bed on the floor. The man turns over from the wall and looks up. McLeod, a small, wiry man, barefooted, bearded, in oil-stained shirt and shorts, gets up from his bed and finds a box for me to sit on.

It is not long before he begins his story of his long and bitter fight with the authorities over the Aboriginals. It is the story of his formation of co-operatives that were sabotaged again and again by the white authorities. As the intense little man talks, he re-lives the story. At times, as the intensity of his feelings make him speak in the present tense, I become confused at the order of events.

But the scenes rise before me as McLeod speaks and acts the narrative. I see the large meetings with the Aboriginals and the clashes with the authorities. I hear the speeches and see the differences among the Aboriginal leaders.

'Many times we walked out with just our bare hands,' says McLeod. 'Many times we lived on damper and kangaroo. We can starve with you, McLeod, the Aboriginals said.'

I cannot absorb and follow all his story. The man himself absorbs me as he talks, unshaven, barefooted, begrimed with the dust of the red earth.

A well-spoken Aboriginal girl brings to my tent a billy of tea and a plate of damper. When I tell her that I did not come here to eat what little food they had, she tells me that it is the law of her people to give food to a visitor. An Aboriginal, whose name is Tommy, comes over with an armful of wood. Another Aboriginal, named Punch, brings me a drum of water.

It is night, and there is talking and laughter in the camp. Out of the darkness comes the 'quiet-feller' the Aboriginals told me about. He is a red kangaroo. He takes damper from my hands. He holds the damper in one paw as he eats it. I stroke his fine, soft fur. When he is ready, he bounds off into the darkness and the spinifex.

In the morning most of the men and women have already set off for the different mines in the hills. In the middle of the clearing stands the community kitchen, an open-air stove. Punch is the man in charge of the kitchen today, and he tells me that the men take turns to be 'kitchen-man' for the day.

In a red, sandy clearing under low mundilah trees, old Maudie is sitting down 'yandying' tantalite out of a pile of sand and ironstone beside her. I see that this method of yandying is a tribal method of separating grass seeds from waste matter. Here this ancient method is being used to separate minerals.

Maudie's yandy is an oval, concave piece of galvanised iron. With a constant yandying motion, throwing the sand in the air towards her with a backwards and forward motion, and a sideways motion, Maudie separates the mineral sand into three heaps. An old man, her husband, carries up the raw material. He immerses it in water and washes the earth from it. He spreads the washed material, dark, wet and shining, out on bags to dry in the sun.

Old Sam, Maudie's husband, sits down at a heap of tantalite which Maudie has separated and, with a magnet, starts drawing magnetite out of the heap. He shows me the magnet with the little dark beads and grains sticking to it. Maudie stops her yandying to take up a baby left crying in a heap of blankets and clothes nearby.

I ask old Sam if he can yandy. He says he can. 'Like Maudie?' I ask. 'More better,' he says.

Don is typing in his hut, sitting cross-legged on the sheet of canvas on the ground. He stops his typing and starts explaining to me the geological nature of the country. He picks up a book on geology from the floor, reads an extract to me, then carries on with his discourse.

'In the millions of years of geological times,' he says, 'man is but a speck in time. You try and think of the world before there was any life. Not a tree, not a blade of grass, not a twit of a bird. It's a frightening business to measure man against the age of the earth. We're just a passing shadow against the sun.'

'I was just a bushman,' he says later. 'I'm still a bushman. Years ago I met a man named Fenton who told me that we were not making use of our wonderful Aboriginals. This set me thinking. Later on, I found myself talking to an old

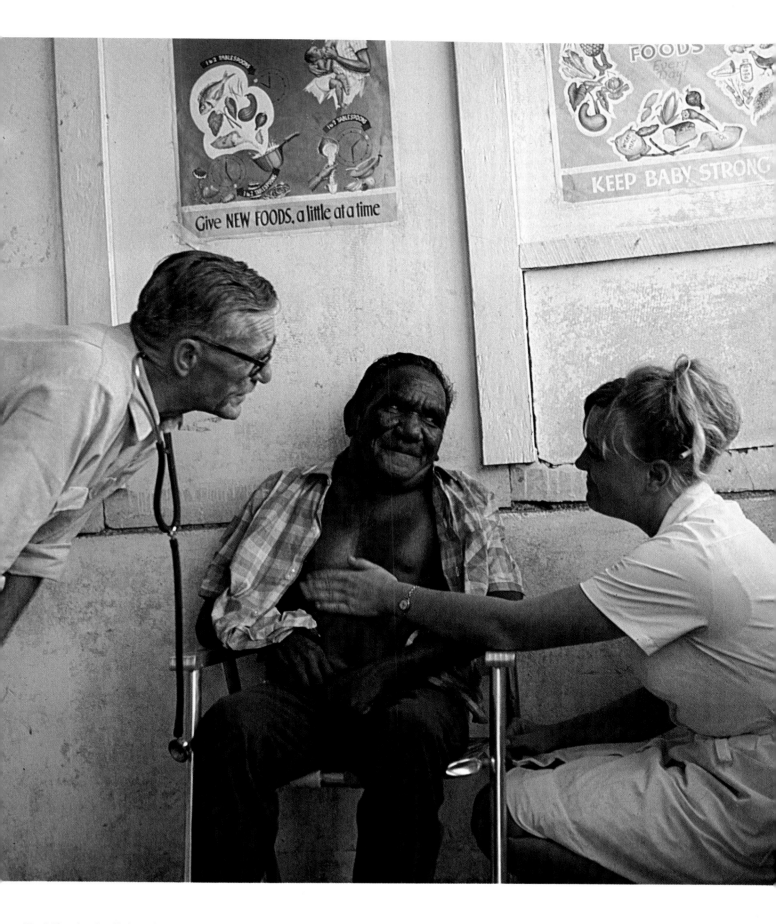

Dr Minnis, the flying doctor at Charters Towers, examines a
paralysed Aboriginal at Weipa.

Aboriginal women dress up to meet aircraft at Weipa, Cape York Peninsula.

Aboriginal woman with cats and hunting dogs belonging to the camp at Tempee Downs.

The advance of civilisation—Aboriginals at a
bauxite reserve, Weipa, Cape York Peninsula.

An Aboriginal stockman outside the stockyards
at Mornington Island, Gulf of Carpentaria.

The tribal Aboriginal in industry. This man, a
bark painter, works at the manganese mines,
Groote Eylandt, NT.

The urban Aboriginal—a family outside their home in Waterloo, an inner Sydney suburb.

Claude Panka, one of the best Arunta artists, at Alice Springs, Central Australia.

An Aboriginal man and woman relax on Bathurst Island, NT.

Aboriginal, the patriarch of his tribe. He reminded me of my grandfather, and I felt like a child as I talked to him. After that I began to take note of the Aboriginals.'

Now he is telling me of the various co-operatives he has started with the Aboriginals. 'There was Northern Development and Mining. It was busted. Then there was Pindan. We had one million pounds in assets when it was busted. I held one share in Pindan. The remaining 6,002 shares were held by the Aboriginals. Our present company is Nomads Pty Ltd. I hold one share.'

A strange Aboriginal has come to the entrance of the hut. 'I'll let you talk in private,' I say, rising to go. 'No, you can stay,' says Don. Then to the visitor he says, 'It's all right. You can talk in front of this man. He's one of our mob.'

This strange Aboriginal has come in from the hills with a sugar-bag of mineral specimens for Don to examine. He empties the bag on the floor and Don examines, assays, and discusses them with the Aboriginal.

I have gone walking through the hills to find the open-cut beryl mine that the Aboriginals are working. In a valley I find the women and children sitting among a scattering of white, broken stones in the midst of the spinifex and the flowers. They are breaking up the white stone with hammers and the backs of old tomahawks. Spinifex has been thrown on low, sparse bushes to make shade for the babies. As I come up to the group, dogs are barking and the *tap-tap, chunk-chunk* of the hammers goes on all around me.

I walk up to the compressor where the men are working. In the open-cut, a white gash in the hill, the Aboriginals are using a jack-hammer and handpicks on the stratum of blue-grey beryl stone. A tall well-built Aboriginal named Jacob is in charge of this mine and he explains the operations to me. They are putting in an explosive charge. I walk away with Jacob through the stones and flowers. Men, women, children and dogs, are walking away through the stones and flowers. Only the 'quiet-feller', the red kangaroo, is staying too close to the open-cut. Jacob calls to him, and then throws stones at him to drive him out of danger.

'*Wham!*' Rocks fly into the air as the charge goes off. Everyone is walking back again. The men start breaking off the 'rubbish' from the fragments of green-white beryl. The women are like *lubras* I have seen sitting and kneeling down as they dig out yams; they are patiently breaking up the stone, talking and laughing among themselves.

I wake in my tent when the sun warms me. The men have left the camp earlier. As I walk across to the community stove with my billy, the women, carrying their babies and small children, are setting out for the mine. They walk in, winding single-file through the spinifex, the tall blue flowers and the scarlet desert-pea against the early sunlight.

The Aboriginal Jack Garden is in attendance at the stove. 'Hard living,' says Jack. 'We live here on damper and tea. But this mine is good for us. We've got a lot of hills out here, a lot of ground to prospect and mine.' He shows me the porridge made out of coarse flour, like chicken food. It has molasses and honey in it. 'When we have no meat this one is good food, makes you feel warm and strong inside', he says.

Don is taking me out to a mine in the hills. He is wearing only a pair of shorts. He picks seeds from the shrubs and grasses and eats them as he walks along. 'The old people made a little cake out of these,' Don says as he plucks something, rubs it in his hands, and shows me the minute, black seeds. 'They yandied to separate the seeds.'

The wild flowers in their profusion made me exclaim with delight. 'Yes, this place is untouched by stock. It's stock that eats the country out. This gives you some idea of what the country was like to the old people before the white man came and made it into a dead country.'

In a dry gully we come on the Aboriginals extracting columbite with tantalite content. Men and women are sitting in the gully bed at work. I did not see them at first, these brown people among the brown earth and rocks. They are yandying the earth, using the wind to remove the dust. A woman stands pouring the mineral earth out of her yandy on to the ground, letting the wind blow away the unwanted earth. I find that a morning's work for one person results in about three fruit-tins of heavy mineral.

'Yandying comes from a method, thousands of years old, for separating seed,' Don explains. 'If you used machinery for this work, it wouldn't be so profitable. You have to make roads for machinery. Here, you just put your yandy under your arm and walk in.'

'Was this the man', I was thinking, 'who had organised the Aboriginal stockmen to strike for decent wages and conditions? Was this the sinister man who had opposed the squatters, the Government, and the police in his fight for the Aboriginals? Was this the man who had been in jail for his actions, who had had a novel and a poem written about him?'

I remembered the first man in Western Australia I had asked about Don McLeod. This was a fisherman on the ocean beach by the Pardoo Sands. 'Don McLeod?' he said. 'I know him all right. He bludges on the Abos. The niggers are no good, not enough intelligence. I've been in Native Affairs, an' I ought to know. They're unreliable, never be anything else than Stone Age nomads.'

I next inquired for McLeod at the police station at Port Hedland. There the police officer informed me, 'I've got a lot of time and admiration for Don McLeod. He's fanatic, but he's got ideals. There's no drunkenness at his camp, and he doesn't live with native women. The squatters are after McLeod because he removed the native labour from their stations.'

As we came down out of the hills, the truck, loaded with Aboriginals, was returning from Roebourne. Jacob, shaved, and dressed in pressed khaki shorts and shirt, socks and boots, came over to talk with me. He asked me how I liked the place. As we were talking, his wife and child came over to us. Jacob was saying that the 'people' of the co-operative liked to have visitors to come and stay with them. 'It means that the white people outside are interested in us,' he said.

'I was working on a station when "The Strike" came on,' he continued. 'That's how I came to be with Don.' Jacob is tall, young and goodlooking, yet now he says that he is getting old. 'And Don McLeod, he's getting old, too,' he added. 'Well,' spoke up Jacob's wife, 'I was brought up in "The Strike", married in "The Strike", and I'll stay in "The Strike".'

As I was leaving in the morning, the 'people' of Nomads Pty Ltd, informed me that they were going to give a send-off sing for me that evening. As I walked out into the starlight, they were waiting for me. On the bare, stony clearing in the middle of the camp we sat down in a half-circle facing the dancers. A brush and spinifex fire was going near us. The songman was beating time with two tobacco tins. He began his tribal song, calling up the dancers.

Almost any cattleman in the outback or frontier regions of Australia will tell you that the cattle industry could not be maintained without the Aboriginals. Aboriginals are excellent stockmen and work in conditions that few white men would accept or could endure. Travelling through the Kimberleys, I had many opportunities to observe them. At the end of one day's drive I camped near a large mob of cattle being settled down for the night. All night I heard the stockmen riding round the mob singing to the cattle to keep them settled and to prevent them from stampeding and breaking back to the country from which they had been mustered and driven.

The singing, coming out of the moonlight and from under the stars, was Aboriginal. Before I woke in the morning the mob had moved on. Later on I caught up with the drovers' 'plant' of horses, donkeys and mules carrying the pack-saddles and with the jangling horse-bells and hobbles round their necks. The man and the boy with the 'plant' were both Aboriginals. They were real stockmen, wearing wide-brimmed sombreros, shirts, jodhpurs, concertina leggings and riding boots. They told me that the mob was being taken to Wyndham. The mob of several thousand head was entirely in charge of Aboriginals. The head stockman was Aboriginal and they had been several weeks on the 'road'.

Later, I stayed at a cattle-camp where all the work of mustering, branding and camp-drafting was carried out by superb Aboriginal horsemen and stockmen.

These men were typical of the Aboriginal stockmen who, in April 1967, walked off Newcastle Waters Station in protest against the judgment of the Arbitration Commission that award wages need not be paid to them until December 1968. After that, similar strikes occurred at Wave Hill, Mount Sanford, and Helen Springs.

To try to gain support for the strikers, two Aboriginals, Dexter Daniells, President of the Northern Territory Council for Aboriginal Rights, and Captain Major, head stockman at Newcastle Waters, made a trip to the southern States addressing numerous union meetings, describing the outrageous food, accommodation and miserable wages paid on the stations in the Northern Territory. They told of the dog kennel-sized humpies of tin and hessian, and of the food that consisted of dry bread and a piece of salt beef.

Under the new award they were paid $14.50 for a seven-day week, ten to twelve hours per day, against a white stockman's $34.50 per week, a five day week and an eight-hour day. As a sidelight the women domestics were paid $4.35 per week, starting work at 4am and finishing at 6pm. What this meant was that Aboriginal pastoral workers were annually having millions of dollars stolen from their pay-packets to go towards extra profits for the pastoral companies. This is still the case.

At this time the Aboriginal secretary of the Northern Territory Council for Aboriginal Rights, Dexter Daniells, sent a letter to the then Secretary-General of the United Nations, U Thant. The letter outlined the plight of the Aboriginal people and concluded: 'After years of degradation and inferiority we have been granted citizenship rights and the right to vote, but this equality is only on paper until we have equal pay for equal work, proper housing, education and training, and some control at least, over our sacred tribal areas.

'There is much more that we could tell you and we can send you further facts on request and photographs of the terrible conditions under which most of our people live.

'We are fighting for our very existence as a people. Please help us in the name of humanity.'

Some years ago, a film was shown on television about a party of Maori people who visited an Aboriginal settlement in New South Wales to give help and advice to fringe-dwelling Aboriginals. The Aboriginals on the settlement wanted a schoolhouse built. The Maori people told them: 'You must do what we did, start with the materials you have here. You have timber growing. Use this.' The import of what the Maori visitors had to say was that the Aboriginal people must begin by helping themselves.

This is precisely what many of our Aboriginal groups are now doing. A few years ago I first visited the Aboriginal settlement at Woodenbong in northern New South Wales. I was, as usual, gathering mythology and at Woodenbong I found many of the traditions intact.

But, socially, I found these Aboriginals living in a state of despondency and apathy. I tried to speak to them of their need to organise and help themselves. They seemed to have neither hope nor initiative. I told them how, when I was travelling to their settlement, my car became bogged. I knew that I would have to get myself out of the bog. I cut bush timber, made a lever, levered up the wheels, and placed timber under the wheels. After several attempts, I brought the car out of the bog.

I remember one Aboriginal, who has been a good friend of mine, replied at the time, 'Yes, but here we're bogged out of sight.'

While I was at this settlement, the people held a meeting to discuss their problems, decide what their aim was, and to arrive at a course of action. I was invited to the meeting at which they decided that what they wanted was land. They wanted the right to farm the land of the settlement as their own co-operative. I then told my friends that they must organise and work to achieve this objective, that they must have leaders and spokesmen. The time had come when they had to take matters into their own hands.

Some time later, two young Aboriginal men, sons of the people I first spoke to at Woodenbong, have been with a deputation of other Aboriginals to Parliament House at Canberra. These two young men obtained an interview with their Minister who told them that the land was theirs. The two young men then asked to have this information in writing. This Minister has promised to act in the interests of the Aboriginal people at Woodenbong.

The Aboriginals themselves have no illusions about the 'Aboriginal problem'. 'It was the white man,' they will tell you, 'who created the problem. And it is the white man who continues to prolong the problem'. It is not merely a matter of educating the Aboriginals, it is also a matter of educating white people to accept the Aboriginals as fellow human beings and fellow citizens. The example of the integration of the blacks in America shows that it is one thing to pass laws but it is quite another matter to cause a white population to recognise and accept these reforms.

On a Commonwealth Literary Fund lecture tour in Western Australia some years ago, I noticed that there were many Aboriginal children attending the primary schools, but I did not find one in the high schools. I brought this matter up in the course of my lectures to adult audiences, and several principals of high schools supported me in my contention that this was not due to a lack of intelligence on the part of Aboriginal children. It was due to the fact that when these Aboriginal children reached the age of puberty they were made to feel the racial discrimination exercised by white children and their parents against them. The Aboriginal children consequently lost interest in their studies and drifted back to the life of 'fringe-dwellers' with their parents.

However, there has been perhaps more progress in education for Aboriginal children in recent years than in many other fields. The old days of a manager-teacher and an inferior curriculum are gone. To see Aboriginal children and white children studying and playing together is to realise the possibilities for the future. In New South Wales the number of Aboriginal children attending high schools is increasing.

Some Aboriginal students have successfully passed through teachers' training colleges, some have entered the nursing profession. The Tranby School in

Sydney trains and educates Aboriginal students from missions, settlements and Aboriginal co-operatives in Arnhem Land and Cape York Peninsula in professions and trades. One Aboriginal who has gained tertiary qualifications is Charles Perkins, and another is Patricia O'Shane.

Albert Namatjira became world famous for his paintings, and the Aboriginal singer, the late Harold Blair, became a teacher at the Conservatorium of Music, Melbourne. During the war of 1940-45, the Aboriginal Reg Saunders was not only commissioned as a captain, but his name is usually associated with those of the famous VCs and great fighting commanders.

Aboriginals have also succeeded in literature. Kath Walker, the poet, has published books of verse which have sold more copies than books by any contemporary poet. The nature of her verse is of social protest for the Aboriginal people and has its roots deeply in the past of the Dreamtime.

Colin Johnson is a young Aboriginal who in 1965 published his first novel, *Wild Cat Falling*. It is the story of an Aboriginal 'bodgie', the dark, troubled, perilous, but not finally unhopeful drama of a youth who, on the morning the novel opens, walks out of his jail in Western Australia to cope once more with the world that put him there.

A young writer who has more recently come into prominence is Kevin Gilbert. In his book *Because a White Man'll Never Do It*, he has done some agonised thinking on the future of tribal and dispossessed fringe-dwelling and urban Aboriginals. He advocates the establishment of 'Black Israels' throughout Australia in which Aboriginals would be, as far as possible, self-supporting. In these areas, he says, Aboriginals would recover their racial pride and identity.

Outstanding Aboriginals such as these have been a vital influence in the present breakthrough or emergence of the Aboriginal people. There are many others, almost unknown who, all their lives, have struggled in campaigns of organisation and agitation for their people. A few such individuals, known to the writer personally, are Mrs Pearl Gibbs of Brewarrina, New South Wales, Charlie Leon, for many years chairman of the Aboriginal-Australian Fellowship, Alexander Vesper, of Woodenbong Aboriginal Settlement, Davis Daniells, Secretary of the Northern Territory Council for Aboriginal Rights, Fred Waters of the Larrakia tribe, Darwin; and Punch, Jacob, Clancy and Dooly of the Aboriginal co-operative in Western Australia.

Today, the Aboriginal people in all States have been granted citizenship rights, constitutionally, at least on paper. In some States there are still discriminatory clauses. The matter of Aboriginal tenure or ownership of reserves and tribal lands is a matter of major concern at the moment. The major breakthrough was the referendum to include all Aboriginals in the Federal census, and to include Aboriginals in all laws, rights and privileges relating to Australian citizenship. The referendum resulted in a 90 per cent vote of 'Yes' in favour of granting these rights to Aboriginals.

10 Black feller, white feller

It is now glaringly obvious to all radical, humane Australians that the 'Aboriginal problem' is not an Aboriginal problem but a white one. It was the white man who created the problem and it is the white man, with his materialistic, predatory values, his ever-increasing demands and needs, who has brought the resentment of the Aboriginals to the surface in outspoken militancy and acts of defiance.

A tradition which I was told of the Dingo-Man and the Macassars, without a doubt could be applied to the white man. The Macassars had landed on the shores of Arnhem Land and had set up their camp. The starving Dingo-Man came along and was offered food, clothing and shelter by the Macassars in return for the right to camp in the Dingo-Man's country and gather bêche-de-mer from the shores. The starving Dingo-Man fiercely refused all their bribes and told them to leave his country and never return; then sat on the shore and watched the Macassars pull up their camp and sail away in their boats.

The hunting and food-gathering Aboriginals, with their weapons of wood, bone and stone, opposed the invasion of the far superior armed white man from the outset. C. D. Docker, in his book, *Simply Human Beings*, records a Queensland tribe which resisted and held up the invasion and expansion of the white man for three years. A narrative given to me at Woodenbong, New South Wales, records organised resistance by the Jabilum Aboriginals at Tabulam to an attack by white men under the leadership of Edward Ogilvie. In this attack a white man was speared to death.

The primitive weapons of the Aboriginals were no match against the rifles and hollow-nosed bullets of the white man. But the aggression of the white man is a deeply seated trauma in the natures of modern Aboriginals. Theirs is a resentment which, although driven deep into their subconsciousness, not only persists, but which is surfacing in a most militant manner today.

It has been my experience that there are many intelligent tribal Aboriginals who are aware of, and concerned about, the predatory nature of the white man. What they, and sympathetic white people, can do to help them in their situation is debatable. I have been given many firsthand accounts by Aboriginal witnesses of genocide perpetrated by the white man through shooting and poisoning. This background must be known and driven home to the white man if the reasons and nature of Aboriginal militancy today are to be understood.

In 1946, a Djauan tribe Aboriginal of the Northern Territory, expressing himself in basic English, informed me, 'Listen, *balanda* (white man), because you come here, bring cattle, build up stockyard, homestead, this is not your country. Every water-hole, plain, river, rock, billabong, is our Dreaming (totemic sites of ancestral beings), belong to my people right back to Dreamtime (Creation time).'

Today, many Aboriginals, some with University degrees, are fiercely articulate. If Aboriginal councillor, Bruce McGuiness speaks in the idiom and spirit of a militant American Negro, it is because many Aboriginal leaders of today have identified themselves and their cause with the Black Power movement of the USA. The white man should take heed, for the Aboriginal cause has become international.

In 1970, Bruce McGuiness made this statement in *The Bulletin:*

> We want our land and the wealth that honkey (white man) dug out of it. We are sick and fed up of being told that we are being helped by the Man (white man), and that the Man is being very generous in giving us this and giving us that. We know that this is a whole lot of toro excreta. All that the Man is doing is appeasing his conscience. He is trying to con himself that he is a good guy. Well, he is only kidding himself, because us black boys aren't buying any of his con.

In 1969, Roosevelt Browne, a black Bermudan Member of Parliament and chairman of the Latin American Black Power Movement, visiting and travelling in Australia, told the Press that if the Aboriginals wanted a Black Power movement they would receive assistance. Warning Australians, he said 'You can never say though, how Black Power is going to work. We hope it's peaceful. But there's no guarantee that there's going to be peace. I haven't heard of any killings in Australia yet, but I wouldn't be surprised.'

The 'Aboriginal problem' is not, of course, confined to the cities. On large outback cattle stations, segregation is rife. I have seen white men who have been working from daylight till dark with Aboriginal stockmen, sit apart from the Aboriginals at mealtimes. At night a transistor may be blaring out its incongruous sounds in the white stockmen's camp while, from the distance, under the stars, can be heard the thin singing, the throb of the didgeridoo, and the sound of the songsticks coming from the camp of the Aboriginal stockmen.

The plight of the fringe-dwellers among the Aboriginals is, in many respects, the worst of all. These are dispossessed, full-blood and caste Aboriginals who live in what are, to us, appalling conditions on the outskirts of country towns.

When I first visited a country town in outback New South Wales I came into contact with the Aboriginal problem there. I was gathering mythology and tape-recording traditional songs. A group of men had sung a song in their own language made many years ago about the shooting of the Aboriginals by white settlers.

I wished to put this song on tape but my Aboriginal friends explained that if I did so the song might be heard by descendants of the early settlers in the district. This, they explained, might cause trouble for them. When I said that these matters should be recorded and explained on tape, one man replied, 'There's nothing to be gained by raking over the past. We want to forget it. What we're concerned about is today and tomorrow.'

This may have been the attitude of the Aboriginals in a country town, but it was not the attitude of the white inhabitants. One enterprising Aboriginal owned and operated a taxi, but he did not obtain any white fares. At the local cinema the Aboriginals sat in a roped-off area and the school near the settlement was a segregated one.

While walking to the settlement one evening (I was barefooted, having taken off my shoes after stepping into a ditch) an oncoming car tried to run me down. To get out of the way, I jumped back into the ditch. When I related this to my friends at the settlement, they said, 'Oh yes, that white man thought you were one of us.'

The dispossessed Aboriginals have cause to be concerned about the present and the future. Their children are growing up in the squalor of the fringe encampments. They will become like their parents, ill-equipped through lack of secondary education and bearing the stigma of the fringe-dweller, with little hope of becoming integrated members of the white community.

In 1961, at the invitation of a manager friend of an Aboriginal settlement in western New South Wales, I made a prolonged stay at the settlement. The telephone was ringing constantly with reports of Aboriginals who had been arrested for drunkenness in the nearby town. There were several cases of Aboriginals being bashed up and seriously injured by the police.

My friend told me that there was little he could do. The previous manager, who had protested about the ill-treatment, had been arrested one evening on leaving the RSL Club in the town and charged with driving whilst under the influence of liquor. He subsequently lost his position. My friend told me that he had sent reports of these matters to his superiors of the Aborigines Welfare Board in Sydney but had received no satisfaction.

A caste Aboriginal who was the handyman at the settlement was to escort some Aboriginal children who were travelling to Sydney for hospital treatment. The manager was taking him into the township and asked me to come along for the drive.

We arrived some little time before the train was due to depart and the handyman asked if he could go and get a cup of tea. The man left us, to my friend's obvious displeasure. The manager told me that the Aboriginal had gone to get a bottle of wine. I was told that when the Aboriginals wanted liquor, it was their practice to go to a restaurant in the town, ask for a cup of tea and, when they paid for it, also tender the price of a bottle of wine. When they had had their cup of tea, they went round to the side of the premises, lifted the lid off a rubbish tin, and there was the wrapped bottle of wine.

I learned that beer, wine, or whatever alcohol they wanted could be obtained after dark by the sugarbag-full. The police would then be informed that the Aboriginals were drinking down by the river and would go down and arrest the drinkers.

On my return to Sydney I was asked by a newspaper editor to write an article on 'The Aboriginal Problem'. I used my experiences in this country town on which to base the article. After the article appeared, the newspaper proprietor and I were served with a writ for $20,000 for libel by the owner of the restaurant in the town.

I returned to the town to collect further evidence for the case. In all my interviews with white people it was admitted that the Aboriginals obtained liquor and indulged in wild drinking orgies, but no white person cared to disclose how or where the Aboriginals obtained the liquor.

One white man, a shearing contractor who employed Aboriginals, said to me, 'You are a hundred per cent right in what you say. I bring my Aboriginals into town and it is not long before they're drunk and in gaol. I bail them out, pay a heavy bail, and in half an hour they're arrested and back in gaol again.' Indignant and angry as this white man was, he would not commit himself to give evidence.

The Aboriginals themselves did that. Six men came forward and gave me signed statements on how and where they illegally obtained liquor. These six men came down to Sydney and supported their statements in the Supreme Court. The case lasted a week and a half, during which time it was disclosed that the

Opposite
Bathurst Island women weaving baskets and mats from pandanus palm fibre. These articles are sold in Darwin.

Ken Coburg keeps an eye on young Aboriginal children at Kirinari Hostel, Sutherland, Sydney.

School for Aboriginal teacher trainees in Darwin.

Primary education on Mornington Island; a classroom of Aboriginal children with one white boy and a white teacher.

Power lines and vandalism have destroyed a sacred ground at Heathcote on the outskirts of Sydney.

Ken Coburg explains the significance of the damaged carvings to his family.

Aboriginal reserve at La Perouse, Sydney—opposite historic Kurnell where their ancestors challenged Captain Cook in 1770.

An Aboriginal girl sells boomerangs to white tourists, La Perouse, NSW.

Aboriginals obtained liquor not only from the restaurant but also from the hotels in the town.

The jury returned with a verdict of not guilty. That this town was not an isolated case, but was typical of many country towns, was common knowledge. After the case was decided, I received letters from residents in country towns asking me to visit them and expose similar conditions.

Shortly after this case, legislation was passed making it no longer illegal for Aboriginals to obtain liquor. This was one of the first of recent reforms regarding the Aboriginals. This means that they are legally entitled to indulge in one of the vices of white men, to experience the effects of alcohol on the human cerebellum.

There is a whole range of songs composed by Aboriginals on the subject of illegal drinking. Drinking was their escape from the monotony of lives lived without purpose. A couple of stanzas from a song known and sung throughout the New South Wales outback explains this:

> The people in town just run us down,
> They say we live on wine and beer,
> But if they'd stop and think, if we didn't drink,
> There'd be no fun around here.
>
> Just the other day I heard a woman say
> We're nothing but a bunch of mugs.
> Although we fight and drink, and end up in the clink,
> We're going to cut a rug.

And was it true that the Aboriginals were driven to drinking methylated spirits? Here is a stanza from another song:

> Beer is all froth and bubble,
> Whiskey will make you moan,
> Plonk is another name for trouble,
> But the metho is out on its own.

In an article on the transitional songs of the Aboriginals, Jeremy Becket, an anthropologist, has this to say on the environment of the dispossessed Aboriginals in New South Wales: 'People who have learned to respect and even admire the traditional culture of the Australian Aborigines shake their heads when they see how low contact with whites has brought them. And indeed, the first sight of a humpy camp or a government settlement is a depressing one. Is this all that the white man, so convinced of his cultural superiority, has been able to give the black? The small out-back township, which few Aborigines have ever left, has little enough in the way of amenities, but even so its citizens try to exclude their dark neighbours from its churches, swimming baths, schools and hotels. In such circumstances, the Aborigines are left to create what life they can among themselves.'

The Aboriginal camp on the river near the outback town previously mentioned, was a depressing place. The humpies were often made from opened-out kerosene tins. An imaginative, spirited, Aboriginal girl who, when living on the settlement, displayed a talent and interest in art, was living in a humpy resembling a dog-kennel in the river encampment. She was an unmarried mother.

The instances that have been related may give some idea of the environment from which the Aboriginals have to rise in their attempt to achieve integration in a white society. Legislation alone will not solve the Aboriginal problem. The Aboriginals have not only to overcome a deeply rooted, hard core of racial prejudice on the part of many white people, but they are up against our whole system of materialism and vested interests. In the case of the large grazing interests, the view is that the Aboriginals represent a pool of cheap labour.

Ken Brindle is a young caste-Aboriginal who is typical of the growing determination of the dispossessed Aboriginals to help themselves. In an indignant and eloquent reply to a reactionary article on the Aboriginals by the author Xavier Herbert, published in *The Bulletin* in 1962, Mr Brindle had this to say:

> Nearly every half, quarter, or lesser caste Aboriginal has grown up on a Government reserve, mission station, or fringe settlement because their white fathers, grandfathers, or remoter ancestors just dumped them there with their full-blood mothers when they'd had their fun. They were not taken into their father's white home and recognised as his children, educated, and cared for, but the semi-human blacks, to use Herbert's words, brought them up along with their own full-blooded kids. So we feel, most of us, that we belong with the blacks, not with the whites who ditched our mothers, grandmothers, or great-grandmothers.
>
> Mr. Herbert says the Aboriginal fringe settlement (Boongville) is a state that suits the race so well that they might have stuck to it generation in generation out. Let Mr Herbert tell me what alternative my people had when they were driven off their tribal lands, their society disrupted, forbidden to hunt their food because they might disturb the grazing cattle.
>
> Let him name one town in the whole of Australia that has welcomed them on an equal basis as human beings. When they were evicted from their lands they were given only one choice — to stay and become unpaid workers, except for handouts on the cattle stations, or to be hunted away, or shot, or poisoned.
>
> That was in the past, people say. The past is pretty recent for Aborigines.
>
> All Australians should know these things, and I think every decent Australian will help us. The white way of life is not the only one, and where Aborigines are a large proportion of the community, as they are in the north, they should not be compelled to assimilate.
>
> ... Aborigines, mostly full-bloods, are battling to run their own co-operatives in some of the poorest country in Australia. It's so poor the whites don't want it unless minerals or oil are found there. If this happens, the Aborigines will be tipped out as they have been at Weipa and Mapoon, without compensation, to become fringe-dwellers without hope or help. Is it any wonder that we think it's time Aborigines had a say in their own affairs?

One of the basic issues among the various Aboriginal organisations today is 'land rights'. I first heard this demand made articulate when, in 1959, I was asked by the Woodenbong Aboriginals to hold a meeting outside their settlement grounds. This was done because of opposition from the white manager of the settlement who, among other matters, had accused me of trying to start 'an Aboriginal Mau-Mau'. At this meeting the Aboriginals decided, of their own accord, that their basic need and demand was 'land'. 'Right,' I informed the meeting, 'Now we have to organise and fight to hold on to every inch of your Reserve.'

During this time, Aboriginal Reserves in New South Wales were being filched from the Aboriginals for the benefit of white graziers. This was being done with the approval of the Aborigine Welfare Board which was universally called by the Aborigines 'The Aborigines Persecution Board'. At the above meeting I also told the Aboriginals that it was essential that they begin to find their own leaders and speakers.

Since that time, a whole new generation of militant, articulate Aboriginals have emerged from their 'Slough of Despond'. This move from apathy to militancy is traced by Chicka Dawson, quoted by Kevin Gilbert in *Because a White Man'll Never Do It.*

> Looking back on the movement, from the time we went on the 1963 Freedom Rides to Moree and Walgett, things have changed tremendously. In those days you could only get two blacks involved — me and Charlie Perkins — with a lot of white students on a bus. Today when you ask blacks to move on a certain issue, you can get a heap of them. But not then. Even up to '68 when we tried to march 'em down George Street to support the Gurindji, you could count the blacks on your fingers, or, at most, fifteen or twenty. Now we can muster 600 or more, so the pendulum has swung.

Among the sixty-five organisations interested in the Aboriginal cause, the first militant organisation, The National Tribal Council, was formed. This Council was linked with the World Black Power Movement. It issued a Manifesto which contained the following headings:
1   Federal responsibility and action
2   Land and mineral rights
3   Education
4   Consultation and power
5   Legal aid and protection
6   Health
7   Cultural pluralism
8   Freedom from prejudice
9   Justice and law
10   Employment

The Tribal Councillors regarded the Queen's visit to celebrate the bi-centenary of Captain Cook's landing at Botany Bay as an occasion for Her Majesty's mourning for her black subjects rather than one of celebration.

Younger urban Aboriginals who had attended a Black Power conference in the United States had met members of the Black Panthers. This visit and meeting resulted in the formation of an Australian Black Panther Party in Brisbane in 1972.

These Americanised Aboriginal Panthers declared that most Aboriginal leaders were 'Uncle Toms' — the American equivalents of Australia's early puppet 'kings' which settlers promoted among various Aboriginal tribes.

Neville Bonner, the only Aboriginal to sit in an Australian House of Parliament, and Peter Howson, the Minister for Aboriginal Affairs, were warned by Commonwealth Police that their names were on a death list drawn up by Aboriginal militants. After a violent demonstration in Brisbane during which nine Aboriginals were arrested, and demonstrations by the Panthers that they were capable of manipulating the media, most of them ended up in gaol.

In 1971, an Aboriginal pastor, Don Brady, was awarded a Churchill Fellowship to study problems of indigenous peoples of Fiji, New Zealand and the United States. Brady was in Chicago at the time of the race riots and felt himself converted to the possibility of using violence to bring about social change.

'The present racial situation is going to get worse before it gets better,' he warned. 'Our people won't give up easily. There will be more demonstrations and attacks on both sides, and they will get bigger each time.'

In 1971, the Victorian Aborigines Advancement League wrote to the United Nations on the subject of land rights. Their demands were:

1 That all land occupied by the Aboriginal people of Australia at the present time be turned over to them including the mineral rights pertaining to such land.

2 That all Crown Land not actually in use be returned to the Aboriginal peoples who owned it and who in justice might be recognised as the owners of it today.

3 That just compensation be paid to the Aboriginal peoples in the sum of six billion dollars.

In the following month Mr Justice Blackburn delivered his judgement in the case of Arnhem Land Aborigines versus Nabalco Pty Ltd and the Commonwealth of Australia. These Aboriginals learned that their traditional affinity to the land gave them no legal standing.

Then, on Australia Day, 1972, Prime Minister McMahon told the Aboriginals clearly that they were not going to get land rights.

On this same Australia Day a group of young Aboriginal militants erected a tent on the lawn of Parliament House in Canberra and proclaimed it 'The Aboriginal Embassy'. Bobbi Sykes, a young participant, expressed the significance of the 'Embassy Tent' in these words:

'"The Embassy" symbolised that the blacks had been pushed as far as blacks are going to be pushed. That from now on they are going forward again. Despite people fighting and struggling right across the country, spasmodically, individually, in isolation, the first national announcement that the pushing back was going to stop was the "Embassy".'

Although authority violently removed the 'Embassy', it was re-erected. When, for the last time the tent was removed, Chicka Dixon, an Aboriginal wharf labourer, used a loud-hailer and told his fellow Australians, 'Vote the Government out of office. If you don't want to be part of the problem, be part of the solution.'

Three months later the Liberal-Country Party Government was voted out of office in favour of the Labor Government.

Despite the fact that the Labor Government was opposed by the Senate which prevented it from passing any basic reform bills for which it was given a clear mandate by the people, this Government immediately set about introducing reforms for the Aboriginals. By 1973, Labor had allotted $117 million for Aboriginal welfare. In 1975 it passed the Prohibition against Discrimination Bill, and Prime Minister Whitlam gave almost 2,000 square kilometres of tribal land back to the Gurindji. This was a culmination of nine years' struggle for land rights by this tribe.

The deeply-seated nature of Aboriginal resentment was voiced by Kevin Gilbert in his book. In one chapter he listed Labor's reforms for the Aboriginals from December 14, 1972 until May 1973. This chapter he entitled 'Labor's Santa Claus', and he said:

'Where do you appeal, after all, when you know that the thief is the judge (appointed by Labor)? Like its predecessors, Labor is essentially concerned with the application of band-aids, bigger and better though they are. But the essential thing, the challenge of the regeneration of a race, is not accepted. Black National U recommends that "the only power Aboriginals will ultimately have will be in their ability for political organisation independent of the institutions of government".'

By 1972, the State Governments of South Australia, Victoria, New South Wales and Western Australia had all recognised Aboriginal title to still existing Reserves. In December 1972, the Prime Minister announced the appointment of Mr Justice Woodward, who had been counsel for the Arnhem Land Yirrkala Aborigines, as Commissioner to conduct a judicial enquiry as a first move towards the legal recognition of Aboriginal rights in land.

This appointment met with criticism from Aboriginals. Bobbi Sykes complained at a conference organised by the International Commission of Jurists that the appointment was made without any consultation with Aboriginals. Speaking of Mr Justice Woodward, she stated, 'He's never been involved in any civil rights issue. He has no idea of how blacks think about things and he has, on many occasions, been on the side of the employers.'

Paul Coe, Aboriginal President of the Aboriginal Medical Service of New South Wales, made this protest:

'On land rights, the Government have left themselves a very good way out by saying that land rights is applicable only by providing tribal association with the land. Now it seems to me absurd to expect people in New South Wales to prove tribal association with the land when the express policy has been, over a period of eighty-odd years, with the Mission set-up, to destroy Aboriginal culture and particularly tribal association with the land. The Federal Government says that it will give land rights to the tribal people because they know that they only have to make a few token gestures.'

Charles Perkins, who had reached the second division in the Department of Aboriginal Affairs, suggested that the terms of reference should include fringe- and urban-dwelling Aboriginals in all States.

Labor's Minister for Aboriginal Affairs, Gordon Bryant, believed that the establishment of a National Aboriginal Consultative Committee would bridge this attitude. After his eclipse, the Committee presented the new Minister, Senator Cavanagh, with a constitution demanding almost absolute control of Aboriginal Affairs. Cavanagh's reaction was that unless the group were prepared to be a National Aboriginal Consultative Committee they would not be paid salaries; the Government would fund a National Aboriginal Consultative Committee but not a National Aboriginal Congress.

Eddie Bernell, an NACC member, asked, 'Why can't the NACC be the Congress? We want to run our own lives. We want to manage our own money. It is the white people now who spend at least 75 per cent of the money allocated to Aboriginal Affairs for Aborigines. The white man spends it nearly all on himself. Poor Aboriginals are still living on river banks and being neglected by the Government. The National Congress can do things for our people, but the white boss says, "You are not ready for that yet". He is not ready to give us the money and let us walk on our own land.'

The Labor Government was under severe criticism also in the form of a white backlash. Many white people complained that they were not subsidised in the manner that Aboriginals were. One life-long militant Aboriginal poet informed this writer that the poet was present when NACC Aboriginals were hopelessly drunk on Bacardi rum when entering meetings.

When the Labor Government was infamously dismissed in 1975 and went to the elections, there was a lack of support for it among the Aboriginals but they were soon to learn that the Liberal Government was no 'Santa Claus'.

In 1976, the Minister for Aboriginal Affairs, Mr Viner, announced that planned programmes of the Department of Aboriginal Affairs would be deferred, and that trimmed departmental activities would save Australia seven million dollars.

The interim Woodward Report earned only the contempt of radical, militant Aboriginals. They noted that the report did not recognise land rights on the basis of Aboriginal law. It allowed some communities to control certain areas and then only on certain conditions. Justice Woodward wondered whether Aboriginals should be allowed to decide against mineral exploitation of their land, so subverting the national interest. How much would the blacks' share be, considering the need to keep up the incentive for whites? Should the government search for minerals? If so, and minerals are found, should blacks be allowed to veto the results of a search?

In his book *Because White Man'll Never Do It*, Kevin Gilbert describes his vision of areas in Australia where Aboriginals would recover their racial pride and identity. Writing of this vision, he says: 'It is human values not to starve and neglect your kids. It is human values to work and contribute to your own community. It is human values to keep your house clean. It is human values to stop your kids from dying. It is human values to maintain a level of conduct commensurate with dignity and pride. It was so in the tribe, it is so today if human development is to have any meaning.'

On a note of black despair, but which yet remains a challenging cry to his race to assert itself, he says: 'Where can blacks turn? To whom can they appeal? Where do you appeal, after all, when you know that the thief is the judge? So what is left? Frustration, negation, blind hatred, powerlessness . . . the psychological nadir. Where can blacks go, in Australia today, except to chapter 7?'

Chapter 7 quotes Mahatma Gandhi:

> Where the choice is set between cowardice and violence I would advise violence. I praise and extol the serene courage of dying without killing. Yet I desire that those who have not this courage should rather cultivate the art of killing and be killed, than basely to avoid the danger. This is because he who runs away commits mental violence; he has not the courage of facing death by killing. I would a thousand times prefer violence than the emasculation of a whole race. I prefer to use arms in defence of honour rather than remain the vile witness of dishonour.

At this time of writing, the Minister for Aboriginal Affairs, Mr Viner, has announced major amendments to the Aboriginal Land Rights Bill. These are:

Give the Senate or the House of Representatives power to disallow government decisions overriding refusal by Aborigines to allow mining or exploration on their land.

Spell out guidelines for Northern Territory Legislative Assembly laws regarding traditional Aboriginal rights.

Not require Aboriginal consent for the granting of further mining rights on land which became Aboriginal land between December 1972 and June 4 this year.

The former Labor Minister for Aboriginal Affairs, Mr Johnson, commented: 'The Aboriginal Land Rights Bill was a cynical sell-out to the Country Party and other vested interests in the Northern Territory.'

Because of the past treatment of the Aboriginals, white people have a responsibility and a debt to discharge towards these first Australians. White people are in need of education and enlightenment in these matters. Our Aboriginals desire neither pity nor charity. They desire the opportunity to prove that, given their self-respect, and acceptance by the whites, they can become responsible and valuable citizens.

Further Reading

Baglin, Douglass and Moore, David R., *People of the Dreamtime*, Weatherhill, NY, 1970.

Buchanan, Cheryl, *We Have Bugger All: the Kulaluk Story*, AUS, Melbourne, 1974.

Elkin, A., *The Aboriginal Australians*, Longman, Melbourne, 1973.

Franklin, Margaret, *Black and White Australians*, Heinemann, Melbourne, 1976.

Gare, Nene, *The Fringe Dwellers*, Sun Books, Melbourne, 1966.

Gilbert, Kevin, *Because a White Man'll Never Do It*, Angus & Robertson, Sydney, 1973.

Lippmann, Lorna, *The Aim is Understanding*, ANZ Book Company, Sydney, 1973.

Lippmann, Lorna, *Words or Blows*, Penguin, Middlesex, 1973.

Marshall, Jock and Drysdale, Russell, *Journey Among Men*, Sun Books, Melbourne, 1966.

Reed, A. W., *Aboriginal Fables and Legendary Tales*, Reed, Sydney, 1974.

Reed, A. W., *An Illustrated Encyclopedia of Aboriginal Life*, Reed, Sydney, 1969.

Robinson, Roland, *Aboriginal Myths and Legends*, Sun Books, 1966.

Robinson, Roland, *The Man Who Sold His Dreaming*, Currawong, Sydney, 1965.

Scarfe, Allan and Wendy, *The Black Australians*, O'Neil, Melbourne, 1974.

Stubbs, Dacre, *Prehistoric Art of Australia*, Macmillan, Melbourne, 1974.

Tatz, Colin (ed), *Black Viewpoints*, ANZ Book Company, Sydney, 1976.

Walker, Kath, *Stradbroke Dreamtime*, Angus & Robertson, Sydney, 1972.

Rough shelters of leaves are erected during preparations for a corroboree. Note didgeridoo player, Mornington Island.